Discipline
The Brazelton Way

ALSO BY T. Berry Brazelton, MD

On Becoming a Family
The Growth of Attachment Before and After Birth

Infants and Mothers
Differences in Development

Toddlers and Parents
Declaration of Independence

Doctor and Child

To Listen to a Child
Understanding the Normal Problems of Growing Up

Working and Caring
What Every Baby Knows

Families, Crisis, and Caring

Touchpoints
Your Child's Emotional and Behavioral Development
    revised with Joshua D. Sparrow, MD

Going to the Doctor

The Earliest Relationship
Parents, Infants, and the Drama of Early Attachment
    with Bertrand G. Cramer, MD

The Irreducible Needs of Children
    with Stanley I. Greenspan

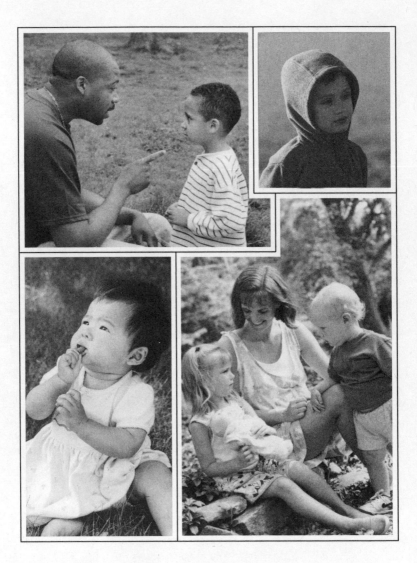

Discipline
The Brazelton Way

T. BERRY BRAZELTON, MD
JOSHUA D. SPARROW, MD

Second Edition

A MERLOYD LAWRENCE BOOK
LIFELONG BOOKS • DA CAPO PRESS
A Member of the Perseus Books Group

PHOTO CREDITS

Photographs on pages xxiv, 32, 104, and title page [upper and lower left] by Janice Fullman

Photographs on pages 56, 142, and title page [upper and lower right] by Dorothy Littell Greco

Photograph on page 78 by Isabelle Bleecker

Photograph on page xx by Marilyn Nolt

Text design by Pauline Brown
Set in 11.5 point Adobe Garamond Pro by the Perseus Books Group

Library of Congress Cataloging-in-Publication Data

Brazelton, T. Berry, 1918-
  Discipline : the Brazelton way / T. Berry Brazelton, MD, Joshua D. Sparrow, MD. — Second edition.
    pages cm
  Includes bibliographical references and index.
  ISBN 978-0-7382-1837-3 (pbk. : alk. paper) — ISBN 978-0-7382-1838-0 (e-book)
1. Discipline of children. 2. Behavior disorders in children. 3. Parenting. 4. Child rearing. 5. Discipline. I. Sparrow, Joshua D. II. Title.
  RJ506.B44B737 2015
  649'.64—dc23

                                        2015009979

Published as a Merloyd Lawrence Book by Da Capo Press
A Member of the Perseus Books Group
www.dacapopress.com

Da Capo Press books are available at special discounts for bulk purchases in the U.S. by corporations, institutions, and other organizations. For more information, please contact the Special Markets Department at the Perseus Books Group, 2300 Chestnut Street, Suite 200, Philadelphia, PA 19103, or call (800) 810-4145, ext. 5000, or e-mail special.markets@perseusbooks.com.
10 9 8 7 6 5 4 3 2 1

Contents

CHAPTER 6 Common Disciplinary Challenges   143

To the children and parents who have taught us so
much through the years

Preface to
the Second Edition

In the more than ten years since the best-selling first edition of *Discipline: The Brazelton Way* was published, our world has been transformed in ways that few of us would ever have predicted. Many parenting challenges remain the same, of course. Yet new ones—along with new opportunities—have arisen across the United States and in the many countries where *Discipline* has been made available in translation. Digital technology and changes in the workplace, families, neighborhoods, and in our increasingly connected planet are reshaping the world in which we discipline our children. These forces are also likely to shape the future for which we use discipline to prepare them.

Despite and because of these changes, parents still clamor for help in responding to their children's misbehavior. It is our hope that this new, revised edition will bring parents the time-tested guidance they need, as well as a commonsense approach to the surprising new twists that they must confront. As with the earlier editions, this one is not intended to cover children's behavior challenges exhaustively, nor to replace firsthand professional diagnosis and treatment.

Information Overload: The Internet

Today, parents seem to be turning less often to parenting "experts" and gurus, though the number of these keeps rising. Instead, parents are connecting with each other. The Internet makes this more immediate and convenient for busy parents than in-person parent groups. Other parents are easier to identify with than "the experts," and may seem more inherently trustworthy, although this may not always be the case. Mommy bloggers, parent chat rooms, and other parent-to-parent sources of information give parents a chance to share challenges and tips, and simply to commiserate, in real time, as a crisis or meltdown erupts.

While parents can do a lot to support each other, and have much valuable wisdom to impart, sharing information through the Internet also brings its own limitations. First, the quantity of information on the Internet can seem nearly infinite, and overwhelming. The overload of perspectives and opinions available online is sure to overwhelm many parents who are just trying to be the best parents they can be. Second, the quality of information is for the most part uncertain and unverified, and parents are left to vet what they read for themselves. Much information—whether from other parents or professionals—is contradictory, rapidly changing, or a matter of opinion. Some of it may be far worse than that, and harmful.

To attract advertisers, websites and online magazines try to create the impression that their readers are all well-off enough to buy all kinds of products. Of course this isn't necessarily true, and an overly rosy portrait is painted of life with young children that makes many parents feel left out, inadequate, or both. While parents may all share common concerns, there are important differences across culture, class, and individual circumstances that often seem to be whitewashed by the commercialization of childrearing. When such tips and advice seem out of touch with everyday realities, they are bound to make parents feel that those who offer them don't understand what raising a child is really like. Parents need to remember that their most important guides will be their child's behavior, their own deepest sense of who their child is, what they want for their child, and the expectations of their family, culture, and community.

Tips and Quick Fixes

Because there is so much more "information" than ever before, and so much less time, much effort is made by parenting media to reduce it to catchy tidbits. These are meant to put busy parents' multitasking temporarily on hold, and to draw them in quickly, before the next banner or alert distracts them away to another website. One result of bite-sized information is that a child's unique individuality is shrunk to fit a label, and a parent's instinctive wisdom is passed over. Children's challenging behavior—which is often a critical communication—is seen as a disturbance to be quashed, before it is understood.

Of course there are many behaviors that must be stopped, and can be. But if they are not also understood, many are likely to reemerge, or to fuel others. As inconvenient or distressing as misbehavior may be, it is also an opportunity. Each behavior challenge is a chance for a child to master, with a parent's help, the job of learning self-control, perspective taking, problem solving, and of developing resilience. Instead, many websites and magazines peddle quick fixes. Promises such as "8 Tips for Taming Tantrums" and "End Sibling Squabbles in 5 Simple Steps" take advantage of parents' understandable desperation, without building on the expertise they already have, and on the special strengths that each child brings to the task of growing up.

This kind of information aims only at extinguishing the immediate problem behavior, as fast as possible. Of course that is what any parent would want, and rightfully so. Yet attention must also be paid to what the child is learning as a result of these methods—"I should do what I'm told because I'll be rewarded, or because Daddy has more power than me"—and to what might have been learned instead. Quick fixes create the impression that "successful" parenting means short-term behavior control, rather than teaching and skill building for life.

Many of the "10 Easy Ways to Stop Your Child's Misbehavior" approaches actually do change behavior—in the short run. It is easy enough to use rewards, bribes, threats, and punishments to get a child's attention, and to get her to stop. They also work well for training puppies. Some of them may have their place. Others may devalue children and parents when they do not spark the child's inner motivation to control her own behavior.

Short-sighted parenting information also reinforces guilt that many parents feel:

- "There are simple ways to control any child's behavior, but I can't seem to make them work."
- "My child's behavior is a reflection on me and my parenting."
- "Everyone else seems to know how to raise children."

This vulnerability is all too easy to exploit. The truth is that parenting, like a child's growing up, is a process of trial and error.

Learning and growth take place through facing mistakes, not in never making any. Any advice, however wise or authoritative, has to be refined and adapted by each parent.

New Pressures, New Trends

Tiger Mothers

There's no short supply of parents and other experts ready to say that their way is best for everyone. Yet the proof is less abundant. A tiger mother's child may compliantly do what she says, and perhaps even gain admission to an elite college. Yet we won't know for decades how they will fare in life or how they'll face its challenges. And we may never know how these children really were raised.

Of course parents must provide expectations and limits. Of course children must learn perseverance and the value of practice and hard work. These do come from struggling through initially difficult tasks that are mastered only with patience and effort. But what else might a successful tiger mother really be giving her children, perhaps without realizing it? If encouragement, hope, and caring are at the heart of her deep investment in them, perhaps these are actually the secret ingredients for their drive and success.

Helicopter Parents

Sometime after the first edition of this book was published, more and more parents found themselves labeled "helicopter parents." Such parents apparently hover over their children night and day, attempting to exert total control over their environment and experience. At times, the label is used when teachers, doctors, and other professionals who work with children want to keep parents out, and don't recognize parents' unique qualifications to understand their children. Yet partnering with parents almost always works better for everyone, especially the children.

Some helicopter parenting may also be due to today's heightened attention to parenting, and greater expectations for parents. Women, in particular, are expected to "do it all"—to succeed in demanding careers while being perfect mothers and partners. But there is no such thing as a perfect parent. Instead, parents all learn to be parents through a process of trial and error, through close and careful observation. Children's behavior is the guide, as well as parents' experiences and the wider expectations of their communities and culture.

Nonetheless, some parental hovering may actually be on the rise. The world may be more dangerous in some ways, and the tolerance for risk is far less than it was when children were given more room to roam. Parents are also aware that their children are growing up in an increasingly competitive and overpopulated world with shrinking resources. When there doesn't seem to be enough to go around—whether water, food, shelter, energy, spots on the soccer team, or seats in high-quality schools—parents may feel justified in intervening to make sure that their child does get enough and is not left behind, even if other people's children are.

Many couples are also putting off having a child until later in life, and having only one or two. As a result, each child is felt to be precious in ways that are different from earlier eras. Parents are bound to be overprotective and to underdiscipline when children are few and long awaited. They may also tend to be single-mindedly focused on their own child, and less on all children, shaping their goals for discipline and the kinds of misbehavior they choose to respond to. (This is one of the reasonable concerns of teachers, pediatricians, and others who dedicate themselves to classrooms, waiting rooms, and busloads full of children.)

When parents come together in communities to share and reinforce their values and expectations for their children, they can increase each other's effectiveness by disciplining in unison. Seeking special treatment for an individual child can prevent her from learning the value of hard work and the importance of making her own way. It may also interfere with learning to share, give, and sacrifice. When parents hover, they may prevent their child from experiencing the stresses that she will need to learn to handle on her own. When parents try to protect their children from the consequences of their own actions—for example, hitting a classmate or avoiding schoolwork—they are interfering with the role that the outside world plays in helping children learn to control themselves. Later on, when parents can't be present and can't insert themselves in these ways, older children and adolescents may flounder and find it hard to fit in.

Another reason for more parental hovering today is that humans have not evolved to raise children alone or in nuclear families. For most of human history, parents have raised their children with the help of many others, and still do so in most places on earth. The nuclear family is a relatively recent development that emerged a century or so ago, mostly in the United States and Europe. In recent decades, many parents have increasingly been pulled away from their families by their work. Declining real wages and the resulting need to hold down multiple jobs, as well as digital technology that brings work into the home at all hours, may finally be tipping a precarious balance. As we reach the limits of what one or two parents can do to raise their children by themselves, it is only natural that parents would increasingly seek help in settings outside the family. Whether in doctor's offices, classrooms, or childcare or neighborhood centers, parents may be reestablishing lost traditions of cooperative childrearing, transforming them for the twenty-first century. As parents seek more support by rekindling relationships beyond the nuclear family, sharing the care of their children with others is bound to lead to some temporary challenges in knowing who, when, and how much to trust.

A "Science" of Parenting?

In recent years, "brain science" has been frequently invoked by parenting "experts," who point to the truly astounding growth and growing complexity of the young human brain in the first three years of life. As one of the pioneers in identifying neuroplasticity in infants, I (TBB) am thrilled with the attention that these discoveries, and the role of the earliest interactions in stimulating brain development, have finally begun to receive.

Unfortunately, this recognition of the critical role of the early years for brain development has also added to the pressure that parents feel. Parents and other caregivers have always needed to be present and sufficiently tuned in to engage in predictable, meaningful, and increasingly elaborate communications with babies—from the beginning of life, long before they can speak. The form that these interactions take varies from family to family, culture to culture, and context to context. Yet many parents have been led to believe that early brain development hinges on one right way to raise a child. It is no wonder that parents may feel competitive with each other, and may measure their self-worth through their children's achievements, such as early reading or test scores.

Happiest Kid on the Block Parenting

Another pressure on parents is to produce the happiest kid on the block, and with that comes competition among parents to produce a happier child than the neighbors'. Unrealistic goals like this make it even harder for parents to accept their role as disciplinarians who must inevitably, at times, impose limits and enforce rules that will make their children miserable—temporarily.

Many parents working long hours wish that they could be with their children more than they can, and of course would prefer to have fun together during the time they do have together. They also worry that they are missing out on important moments of their children's lives—the first word, the first step, the first friendship. It is easy to see how parents yearn to see a happy child and want the reassurances that happy moments might bring.

Of course we all want our children to be happy, but this is not entirely up to parents, and we can't possibly expect children, or parents, to be happy all the time. Not only is this goal unrealistic, but it interferes with other important goals: learning to stick to hard work, coping with disappointment and failure, and caring for others who may be less happy. Many moments of happiness are likely to be the rewarding by-products of these.

It is our hope that in the discipline-as-teaching-not-punishment approach of this book parents and children will find, in addition to reassurance, understanding, and plenty of fun, a sustaining joy in their relationships with each other.

Introduction: Your Child's Road to Self-Discipline

Discipline is the second most important gift that a parent provides for a child. Of course love is the first. But the safety that a child finds in discipline is essential, for without discipline, there are no boundaries. Children need boundaries, and find comfort in them. They know they are loved when a parent cares enough to give the gift of discipline.

Discipline is teaching, not punishment. It won't happen overnight. It takes repetition and patience. Parents' long-term goal for discipline is to instill self-control, so that children eventually set their own limits. This will take many years. In this book we hope to give parents a map of the first steps—the "touchpoints" of discipline. By setting a pattern of firm, loving limits in the early years, parents help a child form the internal standards they will need throughout life. Opportunities for teaching discipline begin far earlier than many parents might think—in the very first days of a baby's life.

When parents learn they are expecting, they hardly imagine that there will ever come a time when they must say "no" to this much-wanted child. But somewhere around 8 months of age, a typically developing child makes it clear that she is doing wrong, but knows better. As she heads for the stove on all fours she pauses and looks up at her father's face, knowing where to find his disapproval. She cocks her head to one side, smiles, and lunges ahead, almost sure that her father will follow and stop her.

This is a rite of passage for every parent. The parents' image of their child's innocence is shaken as they face their new responsibility. Providing for the baby's needs and protecting her from the environment is no longer enough. Now they will have to limit the child's desires and protect her from herself! Saying "no," intentionally limiting a child for her own sake—behaving as a parent in a way that causes a child distress but is necessary for her healthy development—is not what most parents had in mind when they first got started. The child's distress is bound to be matched by that of the parents. They must endure the child's anger at them as they realize what their child needs from them, and what it means to be a parent.

We reveal ourselves in the ways we discipline our children. We reveal how we ourselves were disciplined and how we reacted to the kind of discipline we were brought up with, or missed out on. Among the things beneath the discipline we offer our children are our beliefs about what they are capable of, our dreams about whom they will become, and our hopes and fears for the world for which we are preparing them. Our discipline also reflects our society's values, for as parents we know we will be held responsible for our children's "bad behavior." We know that our efforts to raise "well-behaved" children will be judged by others.

Discipline has different goals in different societies. In life-threatening situations, discipline must teach survival skills. Where individuality is prized, parents will use discipline to reward self-expression. Where individual achievement is admired, discipline will be used to reward a child's efforts to stand out from the crowd, and might not be used to prevent her from stepping over others to get there. In societies that expect individuals to place the needs of others above their own, discipline helps a child to understand the demands on her to fit in, but might punish nonconformism and even initiative.

In a society like ours, made of many cultures, parents and professionals may need to understand that disciplinary practices are shaped by culture, and follow—in a clear and consistent manner—the values and traditions of that culture.

Discipline needs to be individually tailored to each child and must strike a balance. Clear, consistent rules and expectations—with firmly applied consequences when these are not respected—are necessary. But so is an understanding of the child's motivations, of what—at each age—she is able to know, of what she can bear to feel. This, of course, is far more challenging for parents than any merely strict *or* permissive approach. But to raise a morally developing, emotionally competent child will ultimately be more rewarding than raising a simply obedient one.

Child development expert Selma Fraiberg said that "a child without discipline is a child who feels unloved." But discipline is not something parents are likely to receive thanks for from their children, unless they can wait until these children experience the joy and challenges of having children of their own.

CHAPTER ONE

The Touchpoints
of Discipline

Discipline, as we've said, means teaching. Fortunately, in the first six years of life, there are unique opportunities for learning. Later some of these lessons may still be learned, but often in more difficult and painful ways for the child. Among the early accomplishments in which discipline will have a key role are:

1. self-control—recognizing one's own impulses—what sets them off, the ways in which they can hurt others, and learning to hold back from acting on them;

2. recognizing one's own feelings and what brings them on, naming them, expressing them, or keeping them under wraps when necessary;

3. imagining others' feelings, understanding what causes them, caring about how others feel, and recognizing one's own effect on others;

1

4. developing a sense of fairness and the motivation to be-have fairly;

5. altruism—discovering the joy of giving, even sacrificing for another human being.

All of these vital abilities will serve a purpose in adolescence and throughout life. They will be more difficult to acquire later. Without them, the challenges of future years will be even greater.

Touchpoints

Throughout this book we'll refer to touchpoints, which are times when a child regresses in anticipation of a developmental leap ahead. These are times when parents are bound to feel anxious, even irritated. The psychological balance of the whole family may fall apart—temporarily. When parents have reassured themselves that the child is not ill, they can stand back and turn over the challenge to the child, or offer encouragement when needed.

Though we specify times when these changes are likely to occur, children whose disabilities affect their development may proceed through these changes at their own pace. For any child, touchpoints are times when a parent will wonder whether discipline is more necessary than ever, or if a little slack is in order.

The Building Blocks of Discipline: First 6 Months

Right from the First: Getting Organized
From the very beginning of life, a baby must learn to use the states of sleep, alertness, and fussing or crying to balance his needs with the demands of his environment. He will learn to get himself to

sleep in order to refuel or to protect against loud sounds and bright lights. He will learn to cry out to make his needs known, and cry differently depending on what these are. He will learn to gaze intently into his caregivers' eyes, letting them know how important they are and learning as much as he can about them. Each baby will strike this balance in his own unique way.

Soothing and Self-Soothing

Some babies quickly learn to soothe themselves with a thumb in the mouth or by fingering a blanket, while others may need to be held or spoken to softly, or rocked. Each one learns to combine his own soothing strategies with those that you as a parent offer. This is perhaps the earliest precursor of discipline and self-discipline. This early learning about handling crying and other states can be a foundation for later learning about managing impulses and feelings. Parenting is a process of trial and error. Parents of newborns soon learn not to react immediately to each whimper with a massive effort to comfort the child. It's wise to lean in and watch briefly to see how your baby handles his distress on his own. Often, you can then settle back, having witnessed your baby's resourcefulness in soothing himself. At other times, you may know within a matter of seconds that the baby will need to be picked up, held, and crooned to softly.

When your baby has responded to your soothing, you may then need to watch again. Is the child ready to sustain his new, more buoyant mood on his own? Or is he destined to fall apart all over again as soon as he is set back down? Perhaps the infant strokes his cheek with the back of his hand. Or he may gaze at the leaves of a houseplant. You might decide to try to settle him back down.

When you do, he may begin to whimper. This time you could try not to pick him up again. You could say, softly, "You can do it.

You can settle yourself. You're alright." If the baby quiets, tell him, "You're doing a fine job." Often the baby will brighten. The two of you can then communicate with gazes, smiles, and babbles.

Connecting and Disconnecting: Letting the Baby Take the Lead

In a minute or two, the baby will look away and seem less animated. Overloaded for the moment, he has already learned to withdraw in order to settle down. If you sense the baby tiring, try to respect his need for this brief rest.

By stepping back briefly like this, you are offering your baby a chance to try out his internal controls. He will turn to you to supply external controls when he needs them. If you provide all the soothing, then there is no learning. If you provide none, the baby will not learn to calm down, or come to a focused, alert state, by himself. Instead, he may learn to handle distress only by withdrawing into himself. Such a limited strategy leaves the infant at risk of becoming unreachable, unable to develop fully.

If a parent does not understand or respect an infant's need, in the first months, for this kind of connecting and disconnecting, then the child will miss out on this first chance to learn to control his levels of excitement. When you tickle and babble together the baby becomes quite worked up. At the peak of excitement it becomes more than he can handle. When the child withdraws, briefly, to gather himself, it is almost as if he were taking his own time-out! Pay attention to these times as opportunities for learning.

Settling into a Pattern

By 3 or 4 months of age, an infant is able to entertain himself by gazing intently at toys strung over his crib, listening to rattles or bells, and even beginning to try to reach for the toys, though he probably won't succeed in grasping them for another month or so. Now he is resourceful enough to postpone feedings for 3 or 4 hours, and can extend nighttime sleep for longer periods. These new feats are not accomplished alone, but with a parent's subtle urgings.

When a baby wakes up, or at the first whimper, try waiting by your baby's crib, watching to see whether he is able to turn to his toys. If he does, then you can quietly pull back. If he doesn't, you can jingle the toys and draw his attention to them. Then stay close by to watch. If he still can't settle, you may need to pick him up and cuddle him. But when he settles, try again to interest him in the looking and listening that will allow him to make new experiences his own. You may feel that you are deserting the baby at a time like this. But the truth is that when you watch closely to see when to pull back briefly, you are helping him to learn to rely on his own resources.

As you can see, before parents even realize that they are providing discipline for a baby, they are making subtle demands on him to adapt feeding and sleeping to a day–night cycle. Before the idea of discipline even comes up, parents begin to push their 3-month-old to use his own resources to get to sleep, to extend the time between feedings, to settle when distressed, to entertain himself when he is bored. These early patterns set up a foundation for discipline, and for a child's readiness to accept it. Even more important, the baby is already learning to use his own resources to adapt to the world.

7 to 8 Months: The Need for Limits Begins

At around 7 or 8 months, a baby who has begun to crawl is a baby already hungry for discipline. He is caught between the attraction of new territory to explore and his parents' stern warnings: "No, don't go near the stove (or the TV or the lamp)." Soon he will learn to expect a response, and will check your face before he makes his move. If your face says "Come back here," he will crawl faster than ever in the forbidden direction—needing to be absolutely certain that you will chase after him. He is learning what the limits are by testing them out.

Can a Baby Be Spoiled?

Some parents worry that a baby who is held too often will become a spoiled child. We do not believe that a baby can be spoiled before 7 or 8 months. Until then, infant and parent are still working far too hard to learn about each other. Parents are still learning to watch for the signs of what the baby can already do for himself. If you feel that you must protect your baby from every moment of distress, you risk interfering with his learning. Instead, stop and watch closely. After a few whimpers, and even a startle, the baby may begin to finger the soft corner of his blanket. He may gaze into your face—and settle.

By 7 or 8 months, babies have begun to learn to regulate their states, to gather up their attention into a penetrating gaze that every parent cherishes, to soothe themselves when distressed, to settle themselves to sleep when fatigued or overwhelmed. They will continue to struggle with these achievements. But babies who are never allowed to soothe themselves or settle on their own—for example, infants who sleep only when put to the breast—are likely to come to depend on being soothed and settled by others.

Teaching Safety

Kitchen safety is one of the first lessons. Try standing by the stove, reaching a fingertip toward it. Immediately pull your finger away, waving it dramatically. "Owww! Too hot!" as you scrunch your eyes and brow in simulated pain. If he must try too, don't allow him to use more than the tip of his finger to touch the side of the stove, and test out the surface with your own finger first to be certain he won't be hurt. Better still, let him feel the hot air before his finger reaches the stove. "HOT!" Make sure he knows this is *not* a game. If you treat such lessons with complete seriousness and firmness, the baby will know you mean it. At this age, of course, a baby can't be left alone near dangers he'll be tempted to test out.

Pincer Grasp—New Power and New Problems!

At about this age, a child develops a skill that only humans and the great apes possess. Putting thumb and finger together to grasp and manipulate small objects, and to use them as tools, gives a baby new power over the world. He is bound to insist on feeding himself, and on hurling hunks of food in all directions. Desperate, a parent will consider reaching for a raincoat or an umbrella. Now is the time for a tarpaulin on the floor, and forget about rugs.

Of course you'll worry whether he'll ever eat enough on his own. But you're sure to lose if you struggle against your baby's determination to feed himself. Give him a spoon for each hand. Then you may have a chance at slipping some food by. If you reach down to retrieve a fallen spoon and offer it again, you will have started a game that your child will certainly exploit. As you groan and bend, and groan and bend, who's in control? When you tire and stop, you have shown him the limit of his power—over you.

Parents can offer food to a child. But they can't make him eat. Like discipline, feeding must become the child's achievement.

Pointing

At about the same time, a baby finds another powerful new purpose for his fingers: pointing. Before a baby learns to point, it is often hard for a parent to read his desires, and frustrating for the child who is unable to express them. Now he simply extends his arm and forefinger to say "Give me that." This is an exciting advance in the baby's ability to communicate. Parents, delighted now to understand the child so clearly, may put themselves at his beck and call. The moment will come, however, when parents must brace themselves and say, "I can't let you have that." Discipline also means helping a child face and master frustration. At this age, distracting the child with an appealing toy may help, though it won't for much longer. Soon he'll be able to keep an image of exactly what he wants in his mind even when it's out of sight. Then the days of easy diversion from frustration will be over. Unfortunately, this often occurs before a baby has learned the new ways to handle frustration that *will* come later, with language.

Stranger Anxiety

With these new powers, a baby this age is ready to face a new dimension of the world: the distinction between the familiar and the strange. He has noticed and responded to differences between one parent and another, and even a stranger for several months. But suddenly the meaning of "stranger" seems to hit him. Whenever one draws near, he will begin to cry, turn away, and pull closer to his parent. The clinging and crying are the regressed behavior that goes along with this touchpoint: a baby's new understanding of people and their roles in his life. Awkward and embarrassing moments are inevitable as he violently rejects wounded grandparents who—with the best of intentions—can't help but intrude further.

This touchpoint is a time when discipline must take into account the developmental capacities of the child. Discipline is teaching, and this is a time to talk to your baby before meeting the new person. You can gently prepare him for his own fearful feelings and reassure him with the positive things that you know about the person he's about to meet. Still, he can't be forced to take in a stranger at anyone's pace but his own. If he is afraid, he deserves comfort. The "stranger" may need to understand that beneath this intense reaction is a new burst in a baby's understanding and intelligence. It will help if you can also prepare the "stranger" to stay low key, and avoid looking the baby in the eye—a surefire way to make any baby this age cry! If the baby can be allowed to get to know the stranger at his own speed, he will learn to feel in control. He will adapt to his new recognition of strange and familiar people that at first is so frightening to him. Manners will come later.

9 to 12 Months: Reading Parents' Faces

By 9 months, a remarkable new development known as "social referencing" is emerging. The baby turns to a parent's face for information that he can now readily decipher—about any event as it occurs, including his own behavior. The timing of this new development couldn't be more fortunate since by now many infants are crawling. After a peak of stranger anxiety, they can now use a parent's nonverbal behavior to reassure and guide them.

As the child crawls toward the dishwasher, for example, eager to play with the forbidden buttons, he pauses and looks up at his parent's face. He can already recognize a stony face that says "no." He may have already learned that the dishwasher is off-limits. But any child so strongly tempted is bound to need to check a parent's face for a reminder, to clear up any confusion his longing has stirred up. The time for discipline has begun in earnest. Until now, distraction usually would suffice. Now, firmness is called for.

In the first years, young children are investing untold energy in facing tasks that, once mastered, are taken for granted: deciphering the meaning not only of language, but also tone of voice, facial expression, and gestures. Parents are helped by realizing just how hard children work at this, how much they have to learn, and how much they count on us to reveal these meanings to them through our behavior. If we do, we can understand their disobedience as their way of learning through trial and error, rather than as personal attacks on us as parents. We can also understand how critical it is for parents to respond with decisiveness to such misbehavior.

In this early period, clear, consistent messages—the same response, in the same situation—matter most of all. If, as the infant crawls toward the dishwasher, his mother smiles ever so slightly at this playful defiance, of course the infant will lurch forward to see if he can reach the buttons. He will do this even if the mother says "Don't touch that" with a mild display of amusement on her face. When she responds in this confusing way, of course he will do it again to try to figure out what she really means. The baby is responding to the parent's mixed message, which in this case was unclear and difficult for the baby to understand. He will keep on trying until her voice says "no" and her face looks like she really means it.

Testing and the Importance of Repetition

Babies need parents to keep saying "no" until a lesson has been learned and no longer needs to be tested. They learn by repetition. Often parents are frustrated, even disheartened, when a baby or toddler engages in the same behavior over and over again to elicit a "no." Since the baby already knows what the rule is, it seems as though he enjoys tormenting his parents. Why must every child test? He tests because he is trying to understand—Is it always "no"? Is it "no" when you say it this way? Or that way? Is it "no" in the kitchen too? Is it "no" when my friends are over or just when we're alone? Perhaps it *is* "no" the first, second, and third times, but not the fourth and fifth. Perhaps, the baby may be wondering, this is a time when my persistence will pay off!

To make matters more confusing, sometimes "no" isn't always transferred from one context to another. Early on, the television knobs seem all the same—they turn or push, and mommy gets mad. But a little later, the baby or toddler will see that one makes the exciting box shriek and boom, another switches in a new picture, and one sends everything inside away. Is it the same "no" for all of these?

"No, you cannot sit in my lap at suppertime." True at home, but not in a restaurant without a high chair, and not at the grandparents' house, where the child is bound to squirm his way out of his portable booster seat to explore exciting new territory, unchildproofed and full of breakable treasures.

"No" may not be the same for the child in question as for other siblings or parents. The baby who crawls toward the television will have to learn that the buttons are off-limits for *him*. He will have to understand that the rules are not always the same for everybody. We are certainly asking a lot of a child this age! (Even parents struggle to accept that fairness does not mean that the same rules always apply to everyone. In some instances each child in a family should have different rules, in keeping with differences in needs and abilities.)

Add to this the inevitable fact that rules and expectations will change as the child grows. "Yes, you can turn the volume knob now that you know how to do it!" "Wow!" this child might think. "Maybe I can handle those knobs on the stove now too!"

Then there is the likelihood that "no" from one adult to another will not sound or look the same, or be about the same thing. From a parent who works at home, "no" may sound worn-out, but from a parent who is away all day, "no" may sound less humdrum, and is likely to command more attention. An older sibling's "no" may sound more raucous, and a grandparent's "no" may come as a complete surprise!

A home-all-day parent may say "no" to almost-bedtime roughhousing, whereas one who has just returned from work may relish it. The parent who worries more about safety may say "no" to rough-and-tumble play. But if the other parent values self-assertiveness as a protection, a child is bound to read the nonverbal approval in that parent's bright eyes and quiet smile. Parents of babies and toddlers are often just discovering differences in each

---

Making Rules Clear and Consistent

1. Decide what your rules are.
2. Adapt your rules to each child's needs and abilities—they needn't be the same for everyone, and you can help each child understand the fairness in this.
3. Make sure you and the other parent agree.
4. Tell your child what the rule is, with words, tone of voice, face, and gestures.
5. Expect your child to try you again.
6. Respond the same way each time. Any variation makes the child curious to see what will happen next time.
7. Expect your child's new abilities to take you by surprise.
8. Plan on reassessing your rules and expectations regularly. As your child grows, you will need to adjust some of these.

other's expectations for their children. Mixed messages are the understandable result. It is easy to see why repetition, consistency, and clear messages are so important for young children when we stop and consider just how much we're asking them to learn.

12 to 14 Months

A toddler who has just begun to walk is both enchanted and frightened by his new mobility. Staggering around a corner, he can make his parent disappear. He is bound to try this out, over and over, at times elated with his newfound powers, at times sobbing for reassurance that his parent is still there. When a child begins to tease by disappearing, he is telling his parents how desperately he needs discipline. He needs to know that he will be kept safe. Watch his grateful eyes look up at you when you chase after him and tell him firmly, "You're going to come back in here with me." A parent learns that discipline is critical when a child discovers new powers but is not entirely sure how to use them safely. Child and parent establish patterns that they can fall back on in years to come.

Temper Tantrums

At some point, a toddler comes to the realization that he can make his own choices. "Will I or won't I?" His decision means little to anyone else. But he cares so deeply, and is so torn, that he throws himself to the floor and wails. In the process, he's bound to push the limits of his parents' tolerance and to scare himself. Because he is frightened of his new powers, it is not enough for him to know that his parents will help him stay in control.

He must learn to control himself. Though the presence of parents during a tantrum is likely to intensify it, they can offer the toddler ways to calm himself. "Here's your soft blanket." "Here's a cool washcloth for your face." "You can listen to your favorite song." Something the child can use on his own is best: "Here's your teddy bear. He wants to make you feel better. He's sorry to see you so upset. He needs a hug." A parent can soothe a child, but a teddy bear teaches a child to soothe himself.

However, a toddler is unlikely to give up a tantrum as long as parents hover nearby. Without realizing it, they are saying: "You can't control yourself." When parents can *safely* walk away, they are saying, instead: "You can pull yourself together on your own."

Sometimes it is not safe to leave a toddler—in an unfamiliar or unchildproofed setting, for example, or when serious harm is a risk. Then it may be necessary to hold him—on your lap, facing away from you, with your arms holding his arms down on his lap (called the "basket hold")—firmly, but without, of course, causing pain. You can even place a leg over his if he kicks (called the "scissors hold"), with just enough pressure to keep him still, and no more. Keep your head back and to one side if he tries to butt. If he tries to bite in this position, secure both of his arms by wrapping one arm around them. Then put your other arm over his shoulder, and reach up to grasp his forehead with your hand. You can put the side of your head next to his, and even gently press his head against yours to keep it still. Be careful not to put any pressure on his neck. Whispering gently in his ear may help. Or try softly singing one of his favorite songs.

The hold must be secure, safe, and pain-free if it is to steady the child. If this cannot be accomplished, or if the need for holding is repeated and prolonged, then it is time to ask your pediatrician for help. Holding a child to settle a tantrum is always a last resort. But be sure to hold and hug your child often, and at more peaceful moments, so that the tantrums don't become the toddler's way of asking for physical contact.

When you must hold an out-of-control toddler, it is essential to remain calm and settled, so that your child can model on your own behavior. Singing softly, rocking gently with him on your lap, you will teach him ways to calm himself. To do this, though, you will need to keep yourself under control.

Once he has quieted, be sure to point out to him all the things he did to calm himself: "You listened to my song. You let yourself relax. You took a deep breath. You rocked yourself with me." The child will be reassured—and ready to give up the tantrums—once he has learned that *he* is in control. The goal here, as with any kind of discipline, is self-discipline.

The Second Year

"I want that NOW." "You can't have it." The toddler grabs the fragile glass paperweight. "Put it back on the desk." Entranced with the object, the child appears oblivious to his father's words. Wisely, the father moves in speedily and extracts the object from the small fingers. The child falls in a heap on the floor. "You can't have it. It might break." More sobs. "I'm sorry I had to take it away from you. But when you can't stop yourself, I need to help you."

After a violent heave of the child's chest, the sobs begin to space out. "It could break so easily. That would make you sad too." The child looks up at his father through his tears. "Would you like a hug?" The child holds out both arms. He's forgotten about the paperweight.

Sometime during the second year of life, a toddler will discover cause and effect. One thing causes another. I drop the paperweight. It breaks. I climb on the coffee table. I fall down and hurt myself. Until this kind of understanding is achieved, a parent must always be present to take the place of the infant's lack of judgment. Even then, however, the toddler will have trouble stopping himself and using what he has learned about causes and effects to guide his behavior when his impulses are in full swing. Mastering this is a long-term goal for discipline.

Impulse Control

Toddlers struggle with impulses. To the toddler, the world makes sense only if he can touch it, taste it, and climb on it. His new ability to get where he wants, in a hurry, seems to fill him with excitement about everything he is about to discover! However, the world is full of things that are dangerous, breakable, too hot to touch, yucky to taste, and everything else that makes his parents frantic. It's only through his explorations that he will begin to learn about them. A toddler often seems like a rocket speeding toward catastrophe—but also toward opportunities to learn about his world—at every moment.

Parents of toddlers are often exhausted. They know that they must be present at all times to serve as the brakes for the young explorer. Discipline at this age is eye-to-eye, hand-to-hand, shoulder-to-shoulder. Words are worth saying, so that over time their meaning will be understood. But alone they can hardly be counted on to slow up a toddler in time.

Discipline at this age is the gradual teaching of control for this young bundle of impulses. Impulse control is not learned in one fell swoop. Parents of toddlers know (and parents of older children are likely to remember) that such episodes are bound to repeat themselves countless times every day. Children this age often need parents to place their hand on the child's hand or shoulder to stop the unwanted action.

The parent with the paperweight briefly tested out the child's response to words alone, and quickly realized that words were not enough. Had he repeated the request several times, it would have been increasingly unclear to the child that his father really meant it. The words would have lost their potential to stand alone, as they should more often in the next year or so. As soon as the spoken instructions went unheeded, this father moved in and stopped the action. Had he stopped there, he would simply have demonstrated that he had more control over the situation than his son did. Instead, he explained why he had to take over. Then he gave his son a moment to relax, before helping him to imagine his own feelings had the precious object been damaged. Most important, he left his son with the feeling that one day he would be in control of himself.

Toddlerhood is a time for holding hands in the supermarket. Think how much impulse control a child has learned by the time a parent can let go of his hand and allow him to stand a few feet away! A child looks dreamily at the pink-fluff cookies on the bottom shelf. "Come on over here. I need you to tell me which cereal you want." The child who is ready to heed such a request can stop his impulse to grab the cookies, consider his parent's demand, change his mind about what he's going to do, and clomp over to assess the cereal situation. Remarkable, if you think about it! And hard work to get there—for the child and the parent!

Any parent can picture the preceding months—a child seated in the shopping cart lurching out precariously, or on his feet straining as his father grasps his hand. Cookie boxes have been grabbed, wrested free, and settled back on the shelf amid tearful protests. How excruciating for a toddler to give up on his impulses!

Teaching Impulse Control to a Toddler

1. Be sure you have your child's attention first. If necessary, firmly put your hands on his face or his shoulders. Look him in the eye to be sure he is focusing on your message.

2. Make clear that the impulse cannot be acted on. "You can't have it." Or if you're a little late, "Put that back."

3. If necessary, physically stop him from engaging in the behavior you have forbidden. (Take away the toy, remove him from the trouble spot, etc.)

4. When possible, offer the child an alternative. "You can have this instead." This is one way to teach problem solving.

5. Make the alternative a take-it-or-leave-it offer, not a negotiation. The offer shows that your main goal is certainly not to make the child miserable.

6. Stay the course.

7. Sympathize with the child's frustration or disappointment. "It does feel terrible when you can't have what you want." You're not teaching the child to give up all of his wishes and dreams, only to hold back on those that can't be acted on. You are not trying to teach him to like all the rules, just to manage his negative feelings about them so that they don't overwhelm him.

8. Help him understand why—in simple terms—his wish can't come true.

9. If, though, you feel you've truly made a "bad call," it can be an opportunity for you to model the importance of admitting mistakes, and apologizing. If this is done without handing over your authority to your child, you both are bound to feel relieved.

10. Comfort him, and offer him your faith that he can learn, little by little, to control himself. Pick him up and hug him.

11. Look for opportunities to help the child save face. When a child is humiliated, he is likely to try as hard—and as secretly—as he can to justify his behavior instead of changing it.

12. When a day is filled with "no's," find something to say "yes" to. This helps a child to see discipline as an act of love, not as a response to something "bad" in him. This does not mean backing down. It's counterproductive—in most cases—to back away from the initial position.

13. Don't take your child's misbehavior personally, especially the repeated testings. If you see these as a personal attack, you are bound to respond with an attack. Instead, look for what he is trying to learn with his misbehavior, so that you can respond with the teaching he needs.
14. Share this responsibility for discipline, and for teaching, with the other adults in your child's life.

How difficult for a parent to give a child the hope to control his impulses someday, even to believe that it could be worth giving up on all those powerful desires!

Self-discipline means not only that a child can control himself, but also that a child is motivated to control himself because of what this means to him, not just to others. Having learned self-discipline, a child will then be able to balance his needs with those of others. You are laying the groundwork for learning to take place for years to come.

Discipline and a Child's Emotional Development

Understanding Emotions

In order for a child to understand someone's feelings clearly enough to respect them, he must first understand his own. From the beginning of life, a child looks at his caregivers' faces, listens to their voices, and experiences his bodily sensations at the same time. With a familiar face, a familiar expression, a soft voice, responsive to his gazing, to the cycling of his arms, he feels settled, comforted.

Learning about emotions begins soon after birth. Already, a 4-month-old gazes at his parents with such intense interest that he draws them right in to respond. But he is only at the beginning of exploring his role in the feelings of others. When he gets angry and suddenly recognizes that he has made his parent angry, his surprise shows on his face, in his sudden withdrawal, as he turns away. Within six months, he can recognize seven emotions on a caregiver's face—joy, sadness, anger, fear, surprise, distress, interest—and can express these as well.

By 9 months, a baby will expect to find information about any situation on his caregivers' faces. Already, as we saw, he is reading facial expressions to find out what they have to tell about his world. He is learning how important other people are to him—a step in learning to care enough about other people to struggle to please them, and to control himself.

A child's involvement in relationships will propel his learning more powerfully than anything else in his world. He first learns to care about right and wrong in order to please a parent. If discipline is teaching, then every disciplinary measure must take account of the emotional motivation behind all learning. Punishment that leaves a child feeling abandoned, or hopeless about ever pleasing a parent, leaves a child without the emotional motivation to learn from his mistakes.

At ages 2 and 3, a child will often be consumed by conflicting feelings and unattainable wishes. He will struggle to recognize what is going on inside of himself and to know what to call it.

When a child says, "I'M MAD!" or "I HATE YOU!" or "I DON'T WANT YOU TO LEAVE!" or expresses other strong feelings, it is an extraordinary accomplishment! In only a few years, the child has learned to experience emotions, to recognize them in himself and others, and to use language to name them. All these steps are necessary if a child is to learn to stay in control of his emotions.

In order to keep his emotions from overwhelming him, or sneaking up on him and catching him by surprise, or boiling over and undermining his behavior, a child needs to be able to:

- sense his own emotions as distinct sensations;
- notice what ignites them;
- notice what emotions are like when they first start to spark, and when they catch fire;
- learn what he can do to settle himself back down;
- identify what kind of help he needs from others, and ask for it;
- learn to understand what his emotions mean, and to respect and value them.

Dealing with Intense Feelings

The intensity of his feelings is bound to frighten a child and often infuriate his parents. But now he needs his parents' discipline more than ever—to reassure him that he is not endangered by his inner turmoil, that his parents will help him learn to rein in his overwhelming feelings. Parents are likely to be drawn into the struggles he sets up. But he will need to model on their ways of calming themselves, setting the issues straight, and working toward a solution.

Misbehavior is often a child's first try at channeling his intense feelings. For a child to manage his emotions without misbehaving, he will need discipline—and a model in his parent's self-discipline. A child will need a parent's help to learn about his feelings and how to experience them without losing control.

A child's emerging understanding of his own emotions is necessary for him to begin to recognize the existence of emotions in others.

Helping a Child Express and Control Emotions

A parent can help a child:

- feel safe enough to experience his emotions ("I will help you control yourself until you can do it yourself.");
- distinguish different emotions ("Sometimes people feel like being mean when they are scared.");
- recognize the associations between particular emotions and situations ("Aren't you proud of yourself for putting all your toys away!");
- notice and name feelings ("I feel scared in the dark.");
- identify and anticipate triggers ("I hate bedtime.");
- find ways to soothe or express emotions ("I need some books to look at before bedtime." "I'm going to draw a picture of my scary bedtime monster.");
- ask for help managing feelings when he needs it ("Can you sit on my bed and sing our song before you go?");
- accept and value feelings—they are a part of who he is. (A parent might say, "You have so much fun all day. Of course you hate to have to stop at night!" "We love each other so much. Of course we hate to go to bed and have to wait all night before we can see each other again in the morning!")

Recognizing the Feelings of Others

Sometime in the third year, the child makes a startling discovery. For a long time he's been thinking. But now, he can think about thoughts. Few toddlers say, "I thought about that yesterday," or even "I forgot what I was going to say." But some 2- and more 3-year-olds can begin to think about their thoughts, memories, feelings, beliefs, and interests. This leads to thinking about other people's thoughts and feelings: "That baby is crying because he misses his mommy." This new ability is often taken for granted. Yet without it, a child is not ready to learn to shape his behavior so as to take into account the feelings of others.

Discipline will push him to use this new strength, and to anticipate the effects of his behavior. For instance, when a 3-year-old pulls a toy away from his baby brother, making him cry, he might shout, "That's MINE and you can't play with it!" But when their father says sternly, "Do you think he'll want to play with you again if you treat him that way?" he looks up at his father with guilty, but inquisitive eyes. When the father goes on to say, "You know, if you'd offered him something else instead of just taking that toy away, he wouldn't have gotten so upset," the child is ready to think about other people's feelings, even his little brother's. A parent must be ready not just to show a child what he's done wrong, but also positive alternatives.

Empathy: Caring About What Other People Feel

The ability to understand another's feelings and to experience them deeply enough to care has its roots in earliest childhood, though it develops over a lifetime. Sadly, some adults never fully develop this ability. Yet ultimately each person's behavior will not depend on externally imposed discipline (except within prison walls), but on self-imposed discipline. And, in turn, self-discipline is guided by an individual's awareness of and concern for the feelings and needs of others.

Many instances in which discipline is called for are opportunities to teach a child to understand and care about the feelings of others. A 4-year-old is frightened at the sight of a child in a wheelchair. "Look at that boy with one leg," he shouts to his mother. Embarrassed and alarmed, his mother takes him by the shoulders and looks him squarely in the eyes. "How do you suppose he feels to have lost a leg and then have people pointing at him?" The 4-year-old bursts into tears. He has allowed himself to feel the other child's feelings. His mother puts her arms around him and says, "It *is* sad to imagine what it feels like, and scary that this could happen to anyone." This is an opportunity for a parent to change a child's attitude from critical to sympathetic, to teach a child to stop and consider what it feels like to step into someone else's shoes. But this can be painful. Often, underneath a child's cruelty is his vulnerability. Without a parent's support, it can be too painful for a child to face his feelings. Teasing and other negative behaviors are the inevitable result.

Moral Development

Discipline is a parent's way of guiding a child's moral development. With the ability to understand other people's perspectives, a child can see that rules take into account everybody's needs, not just his. When he sees the value of treating others the way he wants to be treated, he'll learn to make sacrifices for others' sake. Still, he'll need self-discipline to follow through.

Before a child is ready to use awareness of other people's feelings to guide his behavior, he will first be guided by other consequences of his behavior. If asked why he wouldn't steal a toy, the 4- or 5-year-old will probably say something like: "The police would put me in jail." Ultimately, though, a parent's goal is to teach a child to behave himself, whether anyone is watching or not. (Soon enough, there will be many times when no one will be!) How does this remarkable transition take place? As parents assure the child that he will face consequences for his misbehavior, they have a choice. They can present the consequence in a manner that asserts their power over the child: "Because I said so" is one example of this approach. Or, they can lay down the law in a way that shows that the "law" is fair, and in everybody's interest: "You know you'll have to give that toy back. You wouldn't want somebody to take your things without asking."

When parents teach their child to obey rules because the rules are fair, and not because the parents are more powerful, they are preparing their child to be law-abiding for the years ahead, when parents will no longer always be more powerful.

Watch a 4-year-old eye another child's tricycle at the park. Unable to stop himself at first, he reaches out a hand to grab the seat. But as soon as he does, he stiffens, looks into the tricycle owner's eyes, and pulls back. This 4-year-old is learning to think about others, and to stop himself. He may be motivated by his wish to make friends with this child, or to avoid his father's scolding. In the years to come, though, he will learn to see that his behavior toward others can take into account their needs and feelings, simply because they matter.

Early on, parents may sometimes be uncertain about the rules that matter to them. This is bound to leave a child feeling uncertain too. Over time, though, as parents make decisions about what their rules will be, their child will need to test these out. When parents respond consistently to this testing, they will help their child settle his confusion. When rules are consistently enforced, a child learns that they don't change to suit whatever a child, or parent, may feel or want at the moment. Consistency demonstrates to a child that rules remain the same because they have their own importance.

Though this will take more time, the goal of parents is to help children use their growing empathy to "do the right thing" for its own sake, even when adults are not there to punish them if they don't. As parents we must help our children find their own motivation to conduct themselves according to a shared moral code. Sooner or later, they will be too old for us always to be present to provide discipline when they waver. By then, we will need to be certain that they have made the values that we have offered them their own.

Self-Esteem

If a child is to care about another, he must learn to care deeply about himself. When an infant is loved, and given opportunities to appreciate himself, a parent is preparing him for empathy. The child's sense of his own value will make it worth his while to curb his impulses for his own sake, and for the sake of others. A child who doesn't like himself has little incentive to care about what happens to anyone else!

Of course love is critical to a child's self-esteem right from the first. But so are opportunities for success, and attention to the development of skills (even more so from kindergarten on) that will help the child to value himself. Less obvious is the role of discipline. A child doesn't like himself when he is out of control. An out-of-control child who isn't disciplined wonders whether his parent believes that he is worth being disciplined. He may wonder if his parents care enough about him to face his anger and frustration when they discipline him. The steadying of one's self-esteem—in the face of both triumph and failure—is a lifelong challenge. The learning starts early.

Excessive demands, even from loving parents, can undo the self-esteem of even the most competent child. He will be at risk of feeling that he is "no good," unable to live up to unreasonable parental expectations. He may even make these his own. When he feels that he can't live up to expectations, his parents or his own, discipline will feel like a criticism.

Excessive demands are a way to set a child up for failure. Punishment rather than teaching—for example, in the form of reproaches, or simply withholding of approval—is sure to threaten a child's self-esteem. Misbehavior can be a child's protest, an attempt to protect himself that is bound to fail. When a parent becomes exasperated with a child's intense and repeated refusal to live up to an expectation, it is certainly time to pull back, reconsider whether the child is really ready, and to readjust the demands.

"I tell you to pick up your clothes and put them away every day and you NEVER do it! Do you want to grow up to be a slob?" one mother angrily shouted at her 5-year-old. A child this age still needs daily reminders for chores like this, or even washing his face and brushing his teeth. Of course this is tedious for any parent, but a child can't yet be expected to organize himself to do these things on his own. It is only through repetition that a child will eventually learn to remind himself. Until then, heavy-handed reproaches are more likely to push a child to rebel against the reminders.

A child who accepts gentle reminders as they are offered, or protests only briefly, is a child who will eventually take them in and make them his own. A child who protests violently may be saying that he is not yet ready for the expectation, or that the reminder feels more like an insult than like help. Some children will even turn their forgetfulness into willfulness, to push away the criticism. A child might answer back, "I didn't forget. I didn't do it on purpose," in order to feel back in control.

Children with challenges that affect learning or social interactions, such as learning disabilities or attention-deficit/hyperactivity disorder, especially when undiagnosed, are especially at risk of damaged self-esteem. If discipline takes the form of harsh criticism, they are bound to protest with "bad" behavior.

Excessive praise, too, can interfere with a child's self-esteem. Too much praise can be hard to live up to, hard to feel worthy of, and hard to take seriously. Some children may need to misbehave in order to test out praise that is too good to be true, or to push parents to shift from overpraising to acceptance of the child as he truly is.

Self-Fulfilling Negative Labels

Children who are struggling to control their urges to hit, or bite, or throw things must be taught to see the effect of their actions on others. When adults use harsh personal criticism, this teaches them instead to believe that they are truly "bad." Such labels can become a child's belief about himself, and a self-fulfilling prophecy. Instead, gather up and hug the child who has attacked. Of course he will need to be told that his behavior is not acceptable, and to face the effects of his behavior. Without this, a child will be left frightened of his own lack of control. He will continue to hit or bite until he knows he can count on an adult to stop him. But a parent must also show love and confidence. The child must learn to believe in his underlying goodness, and in his hope to get himself under control.

Defenses: The Cost of Facing Reality

If a child is to take in the teaching a parent offers about a mistake he has made, he must be able to face his weaknesses. Hard as it is for adults to openly admit their own shortcomings, it is harder still for young children. Their concept of who they are, of their own value, is so much more tenuous. As they grow old enough to realize that they are smaller, less experienced, less knowledgeable, and less skilled in so many areas, a parent's reproaches can feel even more threatening.

A child who believes in himself can dare to face his mistakes. Gradually, he must learn to accept his mistakes, and feel satisfaction when he corrects them. Praise and positive reinforcement can help, but must lead a child toward finding his own pride and satisfaction in his behavior. A child who is dependent on a parent's praise will feel threatened and defensive when it is unavailable or withheld. Over time, a parent will need to substitute "I am so proud of you" with "Aren't you proud of yourself?"

A child's way of protecting himself against upsetting emotions is far less developed than an adult's. When a child must face overwhelming feelings (anger, rejection, fear, and guilt, among others), he often resorts to obvious distortions of reality to fend the feelings off: "I DID NOT STEAL THAT CANDY." But, of course, you know he did.

When we confront a child with his wrongdoing, we are asking him to face his shortcomings and limitations. If, as we point out what he has done wrong, we challenge his still fragile belief in himself and his own worth, he is likely to protect these beliefs—by denying his guilt, by lying, or by listening with only half an ear.

To protect themselves from their parents' reaction, and their own conscience, older children often justify their misbehavior with what they "meant" to do. "I didn't mean to do it. But when I dropped the candy on the floor I thought I'd better eat it so no one else would." Often it is best not to get drawn into legalistic arguments about intent. "It doesn't matter all that much whether

you meant to or not. Your little brother's candy has ended up in
your stomach, whether you meant for it to be there or not. Either
way, you're going to have to take some of your own money to replace it." Offering the child a chance to make reparations and be
forgiven is essential in helping him to face what he has done and
feel good about the outcome.

From Discipline to Self-Discipline

The goal of parents' discipline is to help the child rely on his own
motivation—to control his impulses, to manage his emotions, to
respect the needs, feelings, and rights of others, and "to do the
right thing" for its own sake. As a child grows, parents can leave
more room for the child to recognize his misbehaviors on his own,
the consequences of his acts, and ways to make reparations. This
process begins when a parent notices a grateful look of relief on a
child's face who has just been disciplined. He has begun to recognize he needs it, and is on his way to learning to discipline himself.

Look for opportunities—especially in the midst of a crisis—
for the child to examine and manage his behavior more independently. Substitute "Do you realize what you did?" for "You
shouldn't have done that." Substitute "Do you know how that
made him feel?" for "You hurt his feelings." Substitute "What do
you think you can do to make him feel better?" for "You are going
to have to apologize." These subtle differences tell a child that you
count on him, and that he can count on himself to clean up his
own messes. You are not abandoning him, but letting him know
you value his new strengths.

A child needs to know, and to know that his parents know,
that to make mistakes is to be human. He needs to know that

his mistakes can be understood and forgiven, even though there will be a price to pay. In fact, the consequence can be offered to reassure him that he can be forgiven. Mistakes can be seen as necessary for learning, rather than as a reflection of one's basic self-worth. A child's capacity to believe in his own progress needs to be supported by his parents' faith in him.

Misbehavior as an Opportunity to Teach Self-Discipline

1. Observe your child's nonverbal behavior to see how badly he already feels about what he has done.

2. If he already knows that he's done something wrong, and feels guilty about it, then he's already begun to learn his lesson.

3. When they are too hard to bear, guilty feelings are at risk of being covered over with denial. Don't push the child so far that he can't face what he has done. Instead, commend him for the bravery it takes to face one's mistakes: "I can see you feel awful about what you did. You know I don't want to make you feel worse than you do already." He's likely to be surprised by words like these, and will now be open to listening.

4. If you need to, you can make sure he understands what he's done by asking him to tell you. His words will be worth a lot more than yours, and you'll be able to clarify any misunderstanding you hear.

5. Decide upon a consequence (consult with your spouse if possible) that is closely related to the misdeed, and that allows your child to make reparations. "I'm going to have to hold on to your allowance until you've saved up enough to buy him a new one." "You're going to have to make a nice card for him to say how sorry you are."

6. Make sure he understands the importance of apologies and reparation, and that he feels forgiven. "Do you need a hug?"

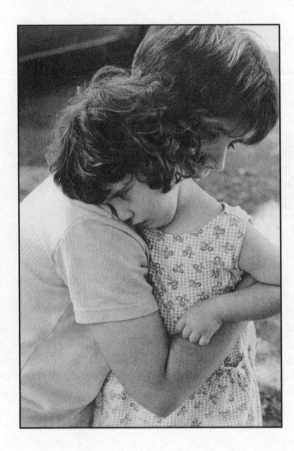

CHAPTER TWO

An Approach to Discipline

In choosing ways to discipline a child, there are two general considerations to keep in mind. First, parents should be aware of the influence of their own pasts. Second, a child's temperament will influence the approach they can take. After discussing these, we will lay out the advantages and disadvantages of different approaches to discipline.

Parents' Memories of Discipline

New parents often remember the ways their parents disciplined them. Many say, "I sure don't want to be like my parents." They may feel strongly about discovering their own ways of disciplining. But discipline is such a powerful part of our past that as parents, we are bound to fall back on the patterns of our own childhoods or gravitate to the opposite extreme.

The moments in which our children call upon us to discipline them are rarely calm or conducive to reflection. A temper tantrum in the grocery store or the backseat of the car in rush hour traffic, someone else's child in tears and brandishing the traces of our child's fingernail on her neck—these are not times for carefully thought-out responses. Instead, we turn without thinking to the most readily available ones, the deeply ingrained disciplinary tactics that we ourselves were brought up with. Tragically, it is no secret that adults who have been abused as children are more likely than others to later abuse their own children. But all of us turn to our own upbringing, whether in crisis or not, to find our way.

Some parents will find comfort and pride in their own capacity to reproduce their family's disciplinary traditions. Others, though, are bound to be chagrined as they find their wish to be a different kind of parent thwarted by their own instincts. For some parents, the frustration that their children stir up in them is compounded by the disconcerting pull back to their own past. Add to all of this whatever immediate worries the child's behavior sets off: Is she safe? Will she get hurt? How will she ever learn to stop herself or to recognize right from wrong? What does this behavior predict for her future?

It is easy to see why it is such a challenge to come up with a disciplinary response in the heat of the moment that cools the immediate crisis yet also reaches for the long-range goals of discipline.

Adapting Discipline to Differences in Temperament

Each child's temperament is unique from the first. The kind of discipline a child responds to and the times when a child will need discipline will vary to some extent with her temperament.

There are three clusters of characteristics that vary with each child and affect how she deals with her world. These, along with the individual rhythms of sleep, hunger, and other bodily functions, define her temperament:

- How a child approaches a task—attention span and persistence, distractibility, and activity level.
- How flexible a child is with people—bold, shy, adaptable, or rigid.
- How a child reacts to sights, sounds, events, etc.—the quality of her moods and intensity of reactions.

A child's temperament is bound to affect what she is able to do easily and what will be a challenge.

- Very active children may have a harder time stopping themselves, and more often need a hands-on approach from parents.
- "Slow-to-warm" children may withdraw, even quietly rebel, when pushed to try something new. They need time to prepare themselves, and may need parents to break down a new demand into smaller steps.
- Very sensitive children, attuned to those around them, may feel responsible for things beyond their years, and be overwhelmed by guilt with even the slightest reproach.
- Children with short attention spans may have trouble carrying out a series of instructions, and may need to carry out one step at a time before being given the next command.
- Children with sensory hypersensitivity are overwhelmed by what they see, hear, or touch. They may need to shut

out sounds or sights around them. This may cause them
to miss out on a parental demand.

Understanding your child's temperament will help you shape
your discipline to be most effective. Discipline adapted to a child's
unique qualities stands the best chance of teaching her to handle
her behavior—on her own.

A child's temperament is also likely to affect her interaction
with parents. "Goodness of fit" is a term coined by Stella Chess
and Alexander Thomas to describe how well a parent's and a
child's temperaments are suited to each other. Battles for control
are a risk when parent and child temperaments are too different,
and parents may wish they could change a child's temperament.
Of course they can't. A parent will do best to accept a child's temperament the way it is, and learn to work with it. Battles like these
are also likely when parent and child are too much alike. Parents
may have to learn to accept their own temperaments when they
see themselves in their child.

The Influence of a Parent's Own Example

Whatever approach you take to a child's misbehavior, you are
offering her a model. My daughter told me about a time when my
then 6-year-old grandson had been doggedly pleading with her
to let him watch "one more" television program. Equally deter-
mined, she held her ground more and more emphatically. When
she began to scream and stomp, the child looked at her and said,
"You know we'll both feel better once you calm yourself down."
At times like these, parents are bound to need a time-out of their
own before facing the child.

Why not let the child know how upset you are and how you plan to deal with it? "I am so upset that I am going to have to calm myself down first, and then take some time to figure out what your consequences will be." She'll know right away that you mean business. Your child will also model on your ability to identify and manage your own feelings. She should be able to count on a fair response to her wrongdoing that is not overly influenced by your initial emotions. But she will need to see how her behavior has affected you in order to learn. A child who has angered a parent needs to learn about the consequences of her actions. But parents can offer a child an important example: they can lay down the law fairly, without acting out of anger even when they are angry.

A parental explosion of anger might frighten a child so much that she would be unlikely to learn. A guilt-inducing response giving the impression that the child has seriously wounded the parent might focus the child more on rescuing the parent than on understanding her wrongdoing. But a modulated and unambiguous expression of what the child has made the parent feel—anger, pain, frustration, fear—will help the child to understand the effects of her actions, and the inner lives of others.

I've watched the Maya people in southern Mexico rely on modeling to raise their children. Their children readily imitate pieces of their parents' behavior. When I attempted to strike up a first conversation with one mother, her little boy peered up at me with bright, questioning eyes. The mother answered briefly, in a low voice, and then looked away. She made it clear that she would have little to do with an outsider. Without a moment's hesitation, the child lowered his lids and turned his head to one side, immediately understanding, and obeying his mother's unspoken message about how to respond to strangers. A parent's ways of handling feelings can also be a model for the child about how to handle her own.

Some parents know they are "yellers" and wish they weren't. Others may believe they are preparing their child for a world where no one is likely to coddle her. Most parents, though, will not want to pay the price for yelling at their young children. Ten years later, they can expect to hear their children yelling back—with the very same tone of voice. Worse still, parents are likely to hear the sound of their own parent's voice (the one who yelled at them) in their teenage child's yelling. Surprisingly, children are often much more likely to stop and listen when parents suddenly lower their voice and speak in a whisper!

The Cost of Humiliation

My grandfather once brought back an antique porcelain doll from China. The neck and shoulders were badly chipped. Its head, mounted to the body on a spring, would be whacked by parents whenever the children who owned it were naughty, according to my grandfather. The damaged doll, displayed in a prominent place in the home, became a symbol that exposed the unforgettable "badness" of its owners.

Is shame a necessary ingredient of discipline? Shame can teach a child to believe she is truly "bad," and to behave that way, or to hide her "badness." Sometimes, it may even put a stop to "bad" behavior—temporarily. But compliance for the sake of avoiding embarrassment simply puts off "bad" behavior until the coast is clear. A parent who shames a child teaches: "Don't get caught." A "public" display of a child's wrongdoings focuses the child on what other people think, when she could instead be learning to consult her own conscience. A child who is punished with humiliation is more likely to be interested in revenge than in apologizing.

Physical Punishment

Spanking and other corporal punishment stop a child's unwanted behavior by frightening a child or causing physical pain, while asserting the power of an adult's greater physical strength. Adults who received corporal punishment as children almost always seem to remember how powerful their parents appeared, and how scared they felt. They also usually remember how angry they were, and how little they admired or respected their parents at those times.

Much less often do these adults remember why they were spanked, or the lesson they were supposed to have learned. One grown woman, now a mother, put it this way: "I remember exactly what I got hit with and where, but I can't remember why. All I remember is how embarrassed I felt, how angry I was at my father, and how much I wanted to get even. But I didn't learn anything." When a parent uses violence to show who's the boss, he or she is saying to the child, "I'm bigger than you are" and "I don't respect you." A child who is treated in this way can be expected to retreat from her parent, and to protect herself within a cocoon of anger. She is bound to lose respect for the adult, and may have trouble taking seriously the moral teachings of a parent who has hurt her.

Spanking is still regarded as an accepted form of discipline by many families in this country and abroad. A generation or so ago in France, many children were brought up in the shadow of the *martinet*, a short, tasseled whip. Perhaps used only once, or never at all, it hung on the kitchen wall as an inescapable reminder of the last resort for "bad" behavior. Sometimes a threat makes the act itself unnecessary. But must a child live in fear in order to control herself?

In other cultures, a wooden spoon or paddle is set aside, ready to whack the bottoms of misbehaving children. Even if never used, it too is referred to, when needed, as a reminder of consequences to be avoided. Many parents never hit their children. They simply remind their children of their power and willingness to do so. Children who can take in this idea, imagine what it would be like, and decide that further misbehavior is not worth it, may never have to experience the reality. But this method leaves a child dependent on parents' threats of physical harm in order to stop and think about her behavior. Parents who had been brought up with corporal punishment are likely to continue the tradition in the next generation. A preschool teacher we know hears some parents say: "My parents spanked me and I don't think I turned out so bad." To them she replies: "You've got it wrong. You turned out alright *in spite* of being spanked!"

Parents who want to raise their children differently from the way they were raised may still find themselves resorting to familiar and deeply ingrained reactions in the heat of the moment. But when they do, they are likely to be overcome with guilt. Those who do manage to steer clear of corporal punishment are more likely to succeed if they prepare themselves with other simple responses that they can call upon when there is barely time to think.

Any family will need to understand its own disciplinary traditions (including corporal punishment), whether they carry them on or take a new course. Family traditions deserve respect, although there are lines that should no longer be crossed. Certainly, bodily harm is unacceptable under any circumstances. But what about transient physical pain—as with spanking or slapping? What about emotional pain, transient or not—as with shaming, humiliating, destructive criticism, or negative comparisons to other siblings? If discipline is teaching and the goal is self-discipline, then these approaches are at best beside the point, and at worst counter-productive. They have no role in disciplining a child.

Parents most often hit a child when they are themselves momentarily out of control. Clearly, there is nothing positive to be learned in this for the child. Much less frequently does a parent hit while calm and levelheaded, measuring out a consistent application of corporal punishment.

When parents use corporal punishment, they are also saying to a child, "You will have to behave because I can make you." These messages do not prepare a child for the day when a parent is absent or can no longer discipline them. In today's violent world, we can no longer afford to teach our children violent behavior. We can no longer afford to discipline them without giving them better and longer-lasting reasons to take responsibility for their behavior. (See "Spanking" on page 97 in chapter 4.)

Getting a Child's Attention

To reach a child who is wrapped up in the midst of naughtiness:

- Use an element of surprise.
- Try lowering your voice suddenly to a whisper, or suddenly shouting a couple of words loudly, for the briefest of moments.
- Try clapping your hands, or a sudden loud whistle.
- Walk away if the situation permits. This will keep you from reinforcing the misbehavior by your presence and involvement. But avoid punishing with withdrawal or threats of leaving.

- If you cannot leave, stop the action by taking the child's head between your hands or putting your hands firmly on the child's shoulders.
- Make eye contact and insist that the child listen. You may need to hold the child firmly, but without applying pressure or causing pain: "I need to stop you until you can stop yourself." A child will give up on trying to upset parents who remain unflappable and will model on their calmness.

For a toddler, these can be simplified into three short steps:

1. "Stop pulling on the tablecloth (or grabbing the cell phone, etc.)."
2. "You need to listen. Stop pulling on the tablecloth"— name the action again—"or I'll have to help you stop yourself."
3. Stand up and move toward the child as you start to say, "I'm going to help you stop yourself."

You should cut the three steps down to one when misbehavior is dangerous or damaging and must be stopped instantly. There is rarely a reason to extend to four or five. If you keep on, the child will simply wonder whether you really mean it.

Reading a Child's Behavior

The degree to which a child is worked up and out of control will also influence a parent's response. A careful look at the child's behavior will help a parent to know when a simple disapproving glance is enough, when a few words are needed, or when to spring into action. Watch and see if the child stops, or begins to slow down, as you start to stand up, before you even get over to her. Often, simply arriving at the scene slows down the action.

Watch to see if the child is completely driven in this moment by her impulse and doesn't seem to take in what you've said until your hands are on hers. Once the child has stopped, settled down, and engaged more or less calmly with you, explain what was wrong about the behavior and why you needed to help. Let her know that you can see she is working on listening, on getting herself under control. Most importantly, make sure she knows that you have hope that she will learn to control herself, eventually.

As a child grows, there will be less and less need to intervene physically. A child who is quietly and methodically wreaking havoc—for example, peacefully scribbling in a book—may only need to be spoken to. One who is frantically ripping pages, or has begun to scribble even more emphatically after being scolded, may need to have the book or the crayons extracted from her grasp. Often, the more physical the child's behavior, the more physical a parent's intervention will need to be. When a child is using words and thoughts for her disobedient purposes, a parent's words and thoughts are likely to be enough.

Often, less is more. Use your face. Try speaking more softly, even whispering, rather than more loudly. The goal is to break into the child's course of action, capturing her attention long enough to decrease the intensity with which she is engaging in being naughty. Your disapproval pushes a child to reevaluate her actions. Scrunch up your forehead, knit your brow, and look at her intently. For some children, for some situations, this can suffice.

(See "Step One: Understanding a Child's Misbehavior" on page 57 in chapter 3.)

The Chance to Make Up for Misbehaving

Discipline must allow a child to face her wrongdoing, to make reparations, and to seek forgiveness. If a child breaks something, she can be offered a chance to fix it, or to help make or obtain a replacement. She can offer her apologies. And she can be forgiven.

If a child hurts another child, she can be offered a chance to comfort the other child, apologize, and plan out how she can keep herself in control in the future. She may need to be told "No more play dates" with that child until she has a plan for the next time. Of course it may not work the next time, but someday it will. Apologies and reparations help a child learn about the feelings of others and to care about them. Effective discipline teaches a child what she must do to be forgiven and allows her to believe that she can be forgiven. (See also "Forgiveness" on page 87 in chapter 4.)

The Power of Consequences

An 8-month-old who has just begun to crawl is fearless. If you place a recent crawler this age on a transparent plate of Plexiglas through which she can see that the table on which it is placed drops away suddenly, she'll proceed without hesitating. But after a month of experience with crawling, the same child will stop, look down again, and freeze in her tracks. One month of bumps and scrapes has taught her the first lessons about dangers in her environment, and the consequences of heedlessness. Of course a parent must protect a child from injury. But too much hovering will interfere with the lessons of experience. A parent can look for safe opportunities to let experience teach a child. The lesson that certain actions lead to certain consequences is a vital one for every child.

A young child, however, is bound to be unaware of some of her behavior's consequences. If she already fully understood, then—in many cases—she would have stopped herself, had it been within her power.

Often a child's misbehavior has a purpose, but not one that is immediately apparent, even to the child. The father of one little girl who ran from one room to another, knocking things down, caught her in his arms and said, "Well. That's one way to get my attention." This father continued, "I know you wanted me to play with you, and I wish I wasn't busy right now. But when you run around and tip everything over like that, you know I am going to be too mad to play. And you know we'll have to spend our time cleaning up instead of playing." This father helped his daughter understand what was driving her behavior, as well as the consequences of trying to draw him in with her negative behavior: an angry father and no time to play.

To help a child learn to connect her behavior with the results, parents can choose consequences that clearly result from the behavior. A consequence that is out of proportion or seems unrelated will be confusing for most children and distract them from the lesson to be learned. Consequences that involve taking away an unrelated possession or privilege are an assertion of parents' power. They will not help the child make the connection between what she's done and the results of her actions.

Parents can choose from consequences that affect the child directly ("Go to your room"), her belongings ("That game is going on my top shelf for the rest of the day if you don't clean it up"), her plans ("No trip to the playground this afternoon"), or the people she cares about ("You won't have your friend back to visit again tomorrow if you keep hitting him"). Consequences should be imposed as soon as possible—especially for younger children—if the child is to make the connection between her behavior and the result. Often, though, the misbehavior must first be stopped, and the child and parent may need to calm down first. A parent may need a moment before coming up with a consequence that makes a point, without retaliation. The child, too, may need a break before she is ready to face the consequence.

Many consequences are more convincing if presented positively: "If you get your coat on quickly, we'll still have time to go to Grandma's." "If you help me set the table, then I'll have time to play with you for a little while before supper." "When you ask nicely for what you want, people are more likely to listen." These are not bribes, but help a child anticipate the positive consequences of "good" behavior.

Bribes emphasize parents' power to give and take away, but interfere with learning *why* some behavior is encouraged and other kinds are not allowed. Prizes or special treats may encourage desired behavior. But many actions have little meaning if a child can't learn to care about them for their own sake.

For example, a child who says "thank you" just for a reward doesn't mean the same thing as a child who says "thank you" and is truly grateful. A more satisfying reward, of course, will be the response the child receives from those she has spoken to in this way. When children learn that their behavior brings its own rewards, they can be proud of their own efforts. Each experience will be a step on the road to self-discipline. Bribes doled out by parents are unlikely to foster such independence.

For older children (5 years and up), an allowance can be a useful incentive for positive behavior. It need not be presented as a bribe, but instead as a privilege that can be earned by helping out around the house. If it is understood that certain chores are required in order to earn an allowance, then certainly it makes sense to withhold the allowance until these are done. When an allowance or any other privilege is taken away, it is important to spell out exactly what the child needs to do to get it back. If the punishment lasts too long ("No allowance for the rest of the year!"), it can seem like forever to a child. The child is likely to lose interest in the reward, which will no longer serve as a motivation for better behavior. In the long run, material rewards for cooperating in a family can interfere with the child's pride and sense of belonging.

Avoid consequences that involve withholding what the child needs, such as food. Food is a necessity, not a privilege to be granted and taken away. Mealtimes are special moments for families to come together, not battlegrounds. Also, connecting food and mealtimes with power or punishment may lead to food refusal and other eating problems.

Consequences

Some consequences are the inevitable or likely results of the child's behavior. A parent's job may simply be to point these out and help the child learn to anticipate:

- "If you use it all up now, there won't be any more left."
- "If you keep doing that, it will break, and you won't get another one."
- "If you run on the stairs, you might trip."

(continues)

(continued)

    Others are consequences that a parent can impose, for example, in order to limit the extent of the child's troublemaking, or to help the child learn to limit herself:

- "If you don't put this toy away first, I can't let you take out another one."
- "If you don't put your toys away, they'll have to go in my closet for the rest of the day."
- "If you can't stop yourself from screaming, you're going to have to go in your room and close the door. You can scream there."
- "When you whine for a toy (or candy) at the store, you can be sure you won't get any—this time, or the next."

    Some consequences are the effect of the child's actions on other people or things. Again, it may be enough to point this out or remind a child, who may be too caught up in the action to be able to think about the result—even if she's been told before:

- "If you hurt someone, she won't want to play with you."
- "If you don't ask for what you want nicely, no one's going to want to help you out."

Least appropriate as a consequence is withheld affection. Affection should not be withheld as punishment. It is natural for parents to be angry when a child misbehaves, and important for the child to learn that this is a consequence of her misbehavior. But she will also learn from modeling on her parent's ability to put the anger aside. When a parent stews or angrily withdraws from the misbehaving child, the child may try out other misbehavior to draw the parent in. A child who feels that she has lost her parent's positive feelings for her has lost the motivation to stop misbehaving and to learn from her mistakes.

A child needs to know that her relationships with her parents are sure to withstand her "bad" behavior. When a child needs a time-out, or to be sent to her room, it is to help her calm herself down, or to remove her from the source of frustration. If the purpose is not clear, though, these techniques can all too easily feel like being sent away forever. Any young child's relationship with her parents is so central to her existence that any such threat to it prevents the child from taking in the lesson to be learned. When a child worries that a parent no longer cares for her, she may behave as "badly" as possible, desperate to test out whether her "bad" behavior really will drive her parent away.

The Importance of a United Front

A parent facing a disciplinary dilemma may need to insist on a time-out in order to consult the other parent when both are raising the child. Often, the offending behavior can be put to a stop immediately, allowing the parents to talk out of the child's earshot if there is a chance of disagreement about the reparations the child will be required to make. "You go to your room right now. Your mother and I will have to talk about how you're going to make up for this—we'll let you know."

One of the most powerful revelations for two parents raising a child together is the discovery of each other's pasts—how each was raised by their own parents. They may find it hard to reconcile differences in their past experiences and current ideas about discipline. Early on, children are bound to sense any disagreements, and they will test them. A child who knows that one parent will side with her against the other, or "protect" her from the other's disciplinary measures, is a child who will continue to misbehave. For a moment she may enjoy the reward of the closeness to the "protective" parent, but she will also feel guilty about disobeying the parent who disciplines. Often, the specific consequence that either parent chooses for misbehavior is far less important than the fact that the choice is backed by both parents.

For parents to agree is often easier said than done. What makes it so difficult to hold off on laying down the law until a spouse can be included in the decision? Any two adults who care for a child are bound to be passionate about that child. It is their passion for the child that sets up competition between them, which I call "gatekeeping." As they compete for a place in the child's heart, they are bound to recognize that the parent who gives in will be rewarded with intimacy—in the short run.

But children need the adults who raise them to agree on the rules and the consequences for breaking them. Parents can discuss in advance—and in private—the predictable misbehavior, and agree on their united response. When challenged with new misbehaviors, parents can contain the situation until they have a chance to talk over the consequence to be imposed. As they move jointly to settle the child down, a quick glance between them can be enough to say: "We need to talk about this later."

Reacting to Misbehavior as a Team

1. Stop the action. Use a time-out or instruct the child to go to her room.
2. Take a deep breath.
3. Consult with your spouse, and work out an agreement you can both live with.
4. Together, set up consequences for the child that relate closely to the misbehavior and that aim at your shared goals—such as impulse control, taking into account the feelings of others, distinguishing right from wrong, etc.
5. Let the child know you've spoken with one another and will discuss her behavior with her when she's calm enough to participate.

Sometimes one parent may respond to a child's behavior by setting a limit, while the other parent didn't think a limit was called for. It is almost always best to go along with the initial response, and to plan to talk later on, in private, about how to handle this in the future. If only one parent is present at the time of the problem behavior, then the other parent must, in general, be supportive of the response. When one parent undermines the authority of the other, the child will feel confused, even guilty, and unsure of being protected by parental discipline from her own impulses. At times parents may need to sacrifice the fine points of their individual views on discipline for the sake of working more closely together. Children who sense that their parents generally function as a team know that they have the safety of a family.

Examples of Issues to Agree On

- chores
- allowance
- bedtime and bedtime ritual
- between-meal snacks
- hitting and fighting
- television (time and what gets watched)

Sharing the Care

In any parenting pair, it is likely that one parent will take more of a disciplinarian role than the other. But even if one parent seems to be the disciplinarian, it often turns out that each parent disciplines, but mostly with regard to the issues that each cares about most. If the disciplinarian role is not shared, children are bound to see one parent as "good" and the other as "bad." However, this does not work itself out in any simple way: usually the parent who shuns discipline is ultimately experienced as at least a little unsettling, or even frightening and unsafe. When there are two parents, children need to know that they can count on both for limits. When discipline is not a shared responsibility, parents may be unwittingly setting up expectations in their children that they will take with them into their adult relationships.

As if gatekeeping weren't enough to throw parents into conflict, parents' frustrations with each other often find expression in disagreements about the children. More or less subtly, they may involve their children in taking sides. "I think you push her too hard," one father said to his wife as their 5-year-old daughter, reprimanded for not picking up her toys, sat sulking out of view under the table. He himself had just been scolded for coming home so late again. His wife defended herself: "How will she ever learn to pick up after herself if we don't start now?" Unable to resist, the little girl shouted out from her hideaway: "I don't like you, Mommy!" Now the 5-year-old is not only struggling with her impulse to move on to the next game before cleaning up the last one, but she also senses that her behavior can be a wedge between her parents. How enticing for any 5-year-old already in the midst of "romancing" one parent at the expense of the other! How little cleaning up after herself seems to matter in the midst of all this!

Turning from One Parent to the Other

Sharing disciplinary responsibilities becomes more complicated as children progress through the expected stage of favoring one parent, while rebuffing the other. The 4-year-old boy who is, for the moment, entranced with his mother will want nothing to do with his father. How much harder it is for this child to hear his father tell him: "I'm going to have to take away that toy since you haven't put it away." How much more motivation to disobey! If his mother is seduced, she may try to "protect" him from his father's protests, and his legitimate limits: "Give him another chance. He's just a little boy." If she does, the father's discipline is likely to be experienced as unjustified and even frightening. The child needs both parents to let him know when discipline is appropriate.

Divorce

When parents are in conflict, separated, or divorced, the child's need for a united parental front is not in the least diminished. Yet, in such circumstances, it is obviously much harder for parents to consult with each other about their expectations and priorities, and to decide together on consequences. It is also much more difficult to defer to the other parent's judgment when one parent is alone with the child. When parents in conflict disagree over discipline, a child will quickly learn whom to go to for what. Parents need to work very hard not to lose sight of the child's needs. Discipline problems must not serve as a battleground for the parents' issues.

Help from Others

No parent can provide the discipline a child needs in a vacuum. A child will learn the demands and expectations of her community not only from parents, but also from grandparents and other relatives, teachers, parents of the child's friends, and others. The rules we all live by are made by the communities we belong to—family, neighborhood, social group, country.

When the "outside world" becomes involved, a parent may instinctively wish to protect the child from the consequences of her behavior. But a child will need to face such consequences in order to learn to discipline herself.

"Shhh! You're making too much noise," a woman hissed angrily at two young children with their mother at a movie theater. A parent might be tempted to protect the children, and to answer back defensively, "They're only kids." How confusing for children of any age! Instead, this is a chance for them to face their effect on others. A parent who can say, "She's right—keep quiet!" conveys a necessary message.

The child's world of childcare and school is a major source of rules the child must learn to live by. Some rules may seem to some parents like a matter of convenience for the teachers. ("The children need to nap after lunch" may seem like an excuse for teachers' breaks.) Others may seem to be the result of inadequate material conditions. (Spaces that are off-limits could have meant more room for children had they been childproofed.) But many rules that children (and adults) must abide by are set to deal fairly with conflicting needs and material limitations. School rules are an early opportunity to help children face the necessity of balancing their own wishes with the needs of others. They will also discover the rewards of curbing their own behavior so as to participate in exciting group activities.

Teachers need parents' support for the rules and expectations of the school setting. But it is easy for parents to feel criticized and defensive when teachers must tell them about their child's misbehavior. All parents know their children are capable of misbehavior, but this is harder to face in school settings, where it becomes public, where parents have less control, and where the stakes may be higher.

The gatekeeping we've described between one parent and another is just as common between parents and teachers. Teachers, too, care passionately about their students, though their efforts often go unrecognized. Neither parents nor teachers like to feel that children's "bad" behavior is their fault. When rules at home and at school are at odds, children are bound to be confused. Parents and teachers may point blaming fingers. But when parents and teachers learn to cooperate, they can reinforce each other's expectations for the children.

When a parent is not sure how to respond to a child's behavior, turning to teachers, grandparents, or other parents can help. "She's so mouthy these days. She's always talking back," one father confides to another as they watch their children at the playground. "My daughter does, too," says the other father. "But you have to say something. She has to see how people react when she is sassy."

Parents who meet when their children are young can continue to help each other over the years and into their children's adolescence, when the issues become more complex, and more frightening. It does take a village to raise a child.

CHAPTER THREE

Discipline as Learning: The Five Steps

Although a child can misbehave in all kinds of surprising and creative ways, parents can usually rely on a recurrent pattern of five steps to guide them as they help him learn from his mistakes. First, a child's misbehavior must be stopped. Second, the child may need to regain control of his emotions and calm himself down before he is ready for the next steps. Third, he needs to think about what he has done and understand the consequences, including its effects on others. Fourth comes problem solving, and sometimes negotiation or compromise as a child works toward making reparations. Finally, apologies and forgiveness.

Step One: Understanding a Child's Misbehavior

"Bad" behavior is "bad" behavior. Understanding it does not mean accepting it.

It must be stopped. It is simple enough to stop "bad" behavior in the moment—distraction, bribes, threats, or punishments will usually do. And of course a parent can stop a child by overpowering him. But when there is no learning, the problem behavior is likely to recur. Besides, this won't work once the child is big enough to stand up to the parent.

Instead, when you understand why a child is misbehaving, you can help him understand himself. Then he is far more likely to learn how to stop his own misbehavior before it starts up again.

The Messages of "Bad" Behavior

When a child misbehaves, usually this behavior says something about his feelings, about what he doesn't yet understand, or can't yet do, or something he is trying to work out—with you, or his teachers, friends, or siblings. This does not excuse it. But when you listen to what the behavior is saying, you will find it easier to know how to respond. Here are a few common messages that "bad" behavior can communicate.

Common Messages of "Bad" Behavior, and Simple Responses

Message: The child does not know the rules.
Response: "It is not okay to do that." (Be sure to say it like you really mean it.)

Message: The child is struggling to control impulses, resist temptation.
Response: "You know you can't take other people's things just because you want them. But I'll help you stop until you learn to stop yourself. We're going to go back to the store so that you can return the candy."

Message: The child needs to test the rules to be sure you really mean them, all the time.

Response: "I really meant it." Or: "That is not allowed anywhere, ever."

Message: The child is trying to communicate something, but cannot yet put it into words.

Response: "I know you're upset, but you aren't allowed to hurt your friend. Once you calm down, we can try to figure out what was bothering you."

Message: The child wants attention.

Response: "I'm sorry I didn't notice how bad you were feeling, but wrecking your toys is no way to tell me. You can always ask for a hug—whenever you need one. Sometimes you might need to wait and that can be hard to do. But I know you can learn to wait."

Message: The child is anxious when parents argue.

Response: "Dumping your food on the floor is no way to say what's bothering you. I'll help you clean it up, and from now on, you can cover your ears whenever we start to argue. Then we'll know how it bothers you. Remember that we are not angry about you."

Message: The child is being teased or bullied at school.

Response: "I know you don't want to go to school today. But I don't know why, and I can't help you make it better unless I do. I can't let you stay at home all by yourself, so you're going to have to get out of bed and get dressed. Come eat breakfast with me, and we'll try to figure out why you don't want to go."

Message: The child is bored and hasn't learned to entertain himself.
Response: "I can't let you rip up your books. If you want me to read with you, just ask me, and I will as soon as I can. In the meantime, you can look at the pictures by yourself, or go get your crayons."

How Does the Child See His Own Misbehavior?

No child likes to misbehave, although it may sometimes seem that he does. The following questions about a child's attitude toward his own misbehavior will help you determine the steps you need to take to help him stop and to get himself under control.

First, ask yourself: Does the child know better? For the child who doesn't yet know better already, it is critical to find out what he is ready to learn.

- Is the child too young to understand?
- Does he know what is expected?
- Has he received mixed messages?
- Are the rules too complicated for a child his age?

Then, if the child does know better, ask yourself: What is driving him to misbehave?

- Can he accept the reality?
- Can he hold back on the impulse?
- Does he need reminders?
- Does he need to know you mean business?
- Does he know the consequences?
- Is he ashamed of what he's done? Proud?
- Is there an unintended reward, such as getting attention from you?
- Does he see the rule as unfair? Why?

- Does he just need a time alone with you to cuddle and receive your undivided attention?

When Misbehavior Is Repeated

When a child keeps on repeating the same behavior, this might be because he gets a different reaction each time, and may be unsure about the limit. You can take a look at your response, and those of other adults who care for him, and talk them over so that he can get the same message from everybody, all the time.

When a child keeps on misbehaving, there may be unintended "positive" consequences that motivate him to keep on doing it. For instance, negative attention may seem better to him than no attention at all. Occasionally a parent's feelings about and reactions to his misbehavior reinforce it, leading him to repeat it. For example, laughing at cute or funny behavior encourages him to do it again.

Even when the child knows what he is doing is wrong, he may repeat it because he doesn't know what else to do. Be sure that whenever you set a limit or forbid a behavior, you help him focus on something different that he can do instead.

Learning takes practice, and practice means repetition. Just because you've had to correct a child's behavior dozens of times doesn't mean that he's not learning.

Sometimes, though, when a child repeats a problem behavior over and over and the reasons remain unclear, it may be a symptom of a more serious problem—for example, attention-deficit/hyperactivity disorder, a learning disability, a mood disorder, anxiety, or an autism spectrum disorder—that needs special attention from a mental health professional. In these instances, the child truly may not be able to learn wrong from right, and even if he can, he may still not be able to make his behavior conform to what he knows is expected of him.

A Note About "Manipulation"

When we call a child "manipulative," it suggests that the child is intentionally using unacceptable behavior to gain what he wants. Thinking of a child's behavior as "manipulative" tends to turn parent and child against each other. It doesn't clarify what's really going on or offer solutions to the problem.

Whenever a child's behavior brings to mind the word "manipulative," try asking these two questions to move beyond blame to understanding—and solutions:

Is the problem simply that the child can't have what he wants? If so, he needs to learn to get his feelings under control, cope with his frustration and disappointment, and accept that he can't always have what he wants.

Or is the problem that the child truly doesn't yet know another way of getting what he needs?

Understanding Your Own Reactions to Misbehavior

Your own attitudes will influence your range of responses, and sometimes even the behavior itself. Here are a few questions that may be helpful to ask yourself:

- Are you ambivalent about it?
- Is there something cute or entertaining about what he is doing?
- Is there something about it that makes you proud? ("At least he won't let anybody push him around!")
- Is he acting out feelings that you have but can't express—for example, toward a teacher, another child, or your spouse?
- Do all the adults who care for the child agree that he must stop?

- Did you do it too at his age? If so, what was driving your behavior?

It helps to notice your own feelings about your child's misbehavior—for example, amusement, annoyance, disappointment, frustration, fear, a sense of urgency or failure, or your own loss of control. The feelings his behavior stirs up in you can influence the response you choose. Besides, the child is bound to read your feelings on your face, and these can make the situation clearer to him, or more confusing.

If you're amused, try not to show it, so that he doesn't think his "bad" behavior is a game you want to play with him again and again.

Often, your reaction is based not just on what your child did, but on something far more upsetting that his act reminds you of—for example, your own rebelliousness, or the much bigger troubles of a relative you fear he may take after. Many parents find that they need to remind themselves that a small child's predictable misbehaviors, from biting and hitting to tantrums, do not predict the child's behavior in adulthood.

Of course parents hold themselves responsible for their child's problem behaviors. But if you are too hard on yourself, you may be too hard on the child, or not firm enough. When you can put your own feelings into perspective, you'll be able to find the right balance, and help your child accept his own responsibility for his behavior.

The Causes of Misbehavior

No matter what the cause is, "bad" behavior must stop. Yet unless you and the child can get to the bottom of it and find out what is driving it, he's bound to keep on misbehaving. Here are a few possible causes to consider; it's easy to see how each one calls for different responses:

Cause: Impulsive behavior—he just can't stop himself.
Solution: You'll have to stop him until he can stop himself. Eventually your repetition will help him learn. It's frustrating for everyone, and hard to stay calm. But when you can, it will help him focus on the lesson he's learning instead of your anger.

Cause: Overwhelming feelings: "I'm so jealous of my baby brother that I'm going to take his toys."
Solution: Make reparations—he'll have to give the toys back—but help him understand his feelings, and try to find time every now and then for him to cuddle with you and "be a baby again" too.

Cause: An underlying problem: For example, being unable to express all of his wants and ideas with words because he is too young, or having a speech delay that leads him to hit and grab when he needs to express himself and can't do so with words.
Solution: Comfort him when he is frustrated about not being able to talk. Watch for predictable times when he's bound to explode because he can't express himself. Help him figure out what he wants as you talk with him. Encourage him without pressure to express himself with words and gestures. ("Are you tired of sitting at the table? Are you ready to get back down on the floor?") Ask your child's doctor if he should have a speech and language evaluation. Almost any child who can't put two or more words together by age 2 should have one.

Cause: Parent, child, or both believe the child is "bad" and cannot be "good."
Solution: Make sure the child knows that it is the behavior that is "bad" and that he can learn to act differently. Reward any "good" behavior, whenever it occurs.

Step Two: Discovering What Happened

Where, when, and how misbehavior is discovered, and who brings it to your attention, says a lot about what started it and what it will take to stop it.

Where?

Misbehavior that happens at home when you are there is usually a lot easier to understand and to deal with. It is simpler to stop, make sure everyone is safe, and to find a quiet place where the child can calm down before you deal with what happened. It may be easier to figure out what happened than when your child is at school or playing at a friend's house. Most of the kinds of trouble a small child can get into at home become fairly predictable—for example, hitting, talking back, being mean, lying, taking someone

---

A Note About "Just Trying to Get Attention"

A child's annoying behavior—for example, repeatedly doing something he knows he shouldn't—is often chalked up to "just trying to get attention." Yet no one really enjoys negative attention, and the whole cycle is no more fun for the child than it is for you. Here are three reasons why a child misbehaves to get attention:

- Boredom, that is, a limited ability to entertain himself, or at least to do so in the setting where he is seeking attention—for example, a long car ride or a long wait at the dentist's office.
- Feelings of competition with other people or things—such as a smart phone or a cute younger sibling (see *Understanding Sibling Rivalry: The Brazelton Way*) that seems to be getting more attention.
- Truly needing your attention—for example, he has something to tell you, or he needs your help understanding a feeling that he can't yet put into words, or he just needs to cuddle and know that there are times when you can be all his.

else's belongings, making a mess or breaking things, cheating or not following directions.

Aggression and taking things are common when a child is on a play date at a friend's house. The most common problem in public places is, of course, tantrums. These usually occur because the child is overstimulated, competing for your attention that has to be shared, and constrained by the limitations of the environment, such as the car or the grocery store. Over time, parents can learn to be prepared with consistent responses for these everyday discipline challenges when they can't be prevented.

When?

When a small child misbehaves, he needs to be disciplined as soon as possible. The longer the time between a parent's discovery and the misbehavior itself, the more difficult it may be for the child to connect cause and effect. If a parent doesn't find out until much later, what happened may not be clear. By then, the child may have invented an alternative explanation that he almost believes, and may not be able to remember what was driving him. The time lapse may also mean that the child knew enough to hide what he was doing, and to cover his tracks.

Who?

Who brings the problem to your attention? If it happens right before your eyes, of course, you know your child made no effort to hide it from you. This is always an easier position to start from, although he may be so ashamed, or so worried about the consequences, that he may try to deny the obvious. If, on the other hand, you are the one to discover the "bad" behavior, then you'll have to find out whether he knew what he did was wrong, whether he intended to hide it from you, and whether or not he'll be able to admit to what he did and to recognize that it was wrong. When he does confess, let him know how much you value his honesty.

If a sibling brings the alleged misbehavior to your attention, then you'll need to assume that you may never find out what really happened, and you'll want to avoid getting in the middle of sibling struggles (see *Understanding Sibling Rivalry: The Brazelton Way*).

Unless the specific problem another child tells you about is part of an ongoing pattern of misbehavior in your child, and as long as no one is seriously hurt or in danger, you may often do best to hold both children responsible for learning how to get along on their own. If one or both are all worked up, though, they will first need to be separated, so that they can calm themselves down and get themselves under control. Without getting involved in figuring out who started it, you can walk them through the steps of apologizing, and then problem solving, for example, switching to a different play activity that gives them both a fresh start. It gets more complicated when your child's friend, or that child's parent, or a teacher reports the "bad" behavior. Unless you have clear reasons to doubt the adults, you'll want to be careful not to undermine their authority, since this can backfire into more problem behavior, and behavior that is harder to control.

How?
How did you find out what happened? If the child himself makes it obvious to you that he's done something he shouldn't, then he is probably crying out for limits. If you don't respond swiftly and clearly, he's likely to be confused, and may be left feeling that no one's paying attention. Worse, it may seem to him that no one cares enough to confront him. Repetition of the misbehavior or more serious misbehavior is the likely result.

Step Three: Confrontation, Containment, and Setting Limits

Your first step is always to establish safety and establish calm whenever these are needed. You may need to get your own feelings under control too.

Facing What Happened, Together

If there is no immediate danger, then your first step will be to choose when, where, and how to let your child know that he has done something wrong. In general, the sooner the better, because any delay can lead the child to think that his misbehavior is acceptable. You may need more time, though, if you're not sure what to do to turn the misbehavior into an opportunity for learning. To buy time, you can simply stop the action right away. Then let your child know that you plan to talk about this with him when things have settled down. You may also need to plan a better time and place to talk over what happened if:

- There are others present and confronting the child in front of them would be humiliating for him.
- You are all worn out and need to rest and recover before you can tackle the problem constructively.
- You are in the car, a public place, or other setting where you may not be able to manage your child's reaction.
- You anticipate that other adults—your partner, the teacher, a friend's parents—may have approaches different from yours. It's harder for the child to learn from discipline when the adults don't agree on the disciplinary response.

When you talk over what happened with your child, you'll have a range of choices:

- You might describe the misbehavior yourself.
- You might ask him to describe the misbehavior.
- You can say why his behavior was a problem, and state the consequences that have resulted or are likely to result from it.
- Or you could ask him to consider his behavior, and to offer his own judgment.

Your response will depend on whether you think he knows what he did was wrong and why, and whether he's ready to face it.

- If he doesn't know why what he did was wrong, that is the lesson you'll want to teach him.
- If he did know already, then your job will be to help him understand why he did something he knew was wrong, and how he can stop himself from doing that again.
- If he's afraid of the consequences, you must be truthful about the consequences he will face, but you can reassure him that they will be reasonable and are meant not to punish him, but to help him learn.
- If he just can't let go of what his misbehavior was intended to obtain (a stolen cookie, a victory won by cheating), you'll have to help him learn to put up with the frustration of not always having his way.

What Have You Actually Discovered?

Whether you confront your child with his behavior, and how you do so, will depend on what he's done. These will also depend on what is reasonable to expect from him given his developmental stage (see chapter 1, "The Touchpoints of Discipline"), and on the circumstances in which he did it. Any small child has less self-control when he's tired, hungry, or stressed. However, what's right or wrong doesn't change, and this needs to be made clear to him. What reasonably can be expected from him will also change as he matures.

Picking Battles

Especially between 12 and 36 months, children are likely to get into one kind of trouble or another all day long. Little by little, this is how they will learn to control their impulses, and to distinguish right from wrong. But if they are constantly corrected, or corrected with too much heavy-handedness, they may tune you out and lose their motivation to do better. Of course you'll always stop a child when he can't stop hurting himself or someone else. But some problem behaviors, such as breaking a toy, can be ignored because they produce their own negative consequences.

Step Four: The Child's Reaction

Your child's reaction to being confronted with what he's done may include:

- denial
- loss of control: screaming, yelling, tantrums
- avoidance
- minimization
- blaming others
- acknowledgment
- remorse

Expect predictable excuses:

- "I didn't do it!"
- "She did it!"
- "It's not my fault."
- "I didn't know I was supposed to."
- "It's no big deal."
- "But it's allowed."
- "When someone else does it, you don't mind!"
- "Last time you said I could!"
- "My friend's dad lets him do it."
- "I don't care."
- "You're not the boss of me!"

These will tell you where you and your child must start and where your teaching will need to take him:

- Soothing and comforting to help him settle his emotions.
- Setting limits—clearly stating what is allowed and what is not.
- Dealing with the feelings of shame and fear of punishment that interfere with facing what happened.
- Avoiding and diffusing power struggles.
- Inspiring the child's hope and motivation.

You will find your own words to accomplish this, but as you search for them it may help to try out a few of the following:

- "You and I both know what happened. We're not going to argue about who did what. We just need to figure out how you are going to make up for your part."

- "You know you can't do this. I know you want to and how hard it is to stop, but I can't let you do this. We can work together to help you remember that this is not allowed."
- "You're right. It's not a big deal when you make a mess. But someone has to clean it up. We'll clean it up together. Cleaning up is a good thing to think about before you make a mess."
- "I'm not talking about someone else right now. I'm talking about you."
- "Your friend's dad can decide what his rules are, but in our house this is how we do it."
- "Maybe you feel like saying you don't care right now, but maybe you really do."
- "You're right. You are the boss of you. But when you can't keep yourself under control, I have to help you."

As your child handles his reaction to being confronted with the misbehavior you have discovered, your goal is to help him move from denial, avoidance, minimization, and blaming others to acknowledgement, remorse, and learning from his mistake.

Step Five: Consequences, Reparations, and Forgiveness

Consequences, as we have said above, are not punishment. They are not just behavioral conditioning. They are meant to help a child understand the connection between his actions and their effects, and to motivate him to change his behavior. If they are overwhelming, frightening, humiliating, or out of proportion, the child will be unable to learn from the lesson his mistake can teach him, and he will lose his faith in your moral authority. If consequences help protect his self-esteem, he can focus on what he needs to learn, instead of denying what he has done. The most carefully chosen consequences can help make the problem behavior the child's problem, help him care about the problems his behavior has caused, and to make the concerns others have about his behavior his own.

> Effective consequences are:
> - supplied as soon as possible after "bad" behavior occurs
> - closely linked to the misbehavior, and serve as reparation
> - enforceable
> - fair
> - proportionate
> - small enough for the child to face
> - help the child care and make the concern his own
> - time limited
> - clear expressions of forgiveness, and of hope for growing and learning

Natural Consequences

Much misbehavior will lead to its own consequences. For example, when a child breaks a toy or rips up a book out of frustration, he won't be able to use it anymore. He'll learn to think twice before handling frustration this way again, as long as you don't rush to replace what he has broken. If he keeps on hitting another child, the child won't want to play with him—again a natural consequence that shouldn't be interfered with, except to protect the other child. Your child may, though, need you to help him to see the connection if it isn't clear to him. First, try asking him why he thinks his friend's mother says her son can't play with him, and then supply the missing information if necessary.

It can be tempting to intervene to protect your child from natural consequences for his misbehavior, or from consequences imposed by non–family members or by family members whose expectations for your child are different from yours. This is especially difficult to resist when your child is distraught, and turns to you to make everything better. At times, he may even threaten to never forgive you if you don't. You'll have to decide what to do in each instance, but it may help to remember that reducing your child's distress in the short term may lead to more misbehavior and more distress in the long run. Although it may seem counterintuitive, parents show they really care when they dare to risk a child's anger in order to help the child grow and learn.

As a child grows older, more of his behavior will have consequences in the larger world, and you will not be able to protect him from many of them. Better that you and he get used to this now rather than being surprised later on. In any case, when your child is too big for you to control his behavior, you will have no choice but to rely on external consequences for his actions if he gets into big trouble at school, out in the community, or with the law.

Consequences Help Teach Problem Solving

Many discipline problems arise from children's limited problem-solving abilities. Problem solving is one of the most important skills any of us will ever learn. In fact, it's tempting to think that better problem-solving skills might help with many of the most serious challenges our world must face.

Misbehavior can become an opportunity for children to practice problem-solving skills—with a parent's help. Consequences can also help young children try out better solutions to the problems they face, such as handling their strong emotions, sharing, taking turns, understanding others' feelings and perspectives, making compromises, tolerating frustration, and doing things they don't want to do that still need to be done. Consequences that fit the misbehavior help children feel that they can make things right, and that they can be forgiven. This helps them bounce back, building resilience. They also reinforce a parent's moral authority, one of the most important tools for teaching discipline a parent will ever have.

Here are several examples of problem-solving consequences that fit the misbehavior:

- "You took his toy. Give it back and find something of your own to play with."
- "You broke something on purpose (or carelessly). Fix it or use your allowance to help buy a new one."
- "You broke something when you were angry. Fix it and find something that you can squeeze or tear or throw when you're angry that won't break and won't hurt anyone."
- "You can't stop fighting with each other this morning. Play separately until you're ready to play together and get along, or switch to a game that you both can play without fighting."
- "Next time your little sister interrupts your game, give her something of her own that she likes to play with."
- "You hurt his feelings. Say you're sorry and mean it, and offer a hug." (This solves the problem of how bad both children were feeling, because the child who can sincerely apologize will feel better too.)

Often it's best when you and your child can come up with consequences like these together. Try asking him first how he thinks he can make things better.

Consequences can help show what the problem is and how to solve it, and they help set things right again. Time-outs (unless they are assigned only when the child is out of control and needs to calm down), docking an allowance (unless the child needs to pay for something he's taken or broken), grounding (unless the child has endangered himself when outdoors), corporal punishment, and other responses less specifically tied to misbehavior usually do not teach, even though they may temporarily shut down the misbehavior. If they shame the child, they may convince him that he is "bad." Once he believes in his own "badness," he's then more likely to get himself into more trouble. If the consequences are frightening and difficult to understand, then the child will just be more careful to hide his "bad" behavior next time.

Reparations

Children are most likely to learn from their mistakes if they have an opportunity to repair whatever damage they may have done. Making reparations requires them to overcome feelings of embarrassment or shame, to face the effects of their actions, and to practice problem solving. Often they will need your help in order to figure out how to make things better. That is an important goal for the consequences you choose.

Consequences like these can help a child make reparations:

- Offer the opportunity to face mistakes, accept responsibility, "make up," and move on.
- Help the child see that he can learn from his mistake so that he doesn't have to make the same one again.
- Protect the child's sense of himself: a child who thinks he's bad will expect to misbehave.
- Express forgiveness and hope—that the child can do better the next time.
- Never withhold or withdraw a parent's love.

Forgiveness Fosters Resilience

Once the child has been able to face what he has done wrong and to accept the reparations he must make, it is time to let him know that he will be forgiven. When you forgive your child, you are telling him that his misbehavior does not define who he is, or what you think and feel about him. Forgiveness puts his mistake into perspective. It is a way of telling him that you are ready to move on, and so can he. When you show him that you can let go of your anger, frustration, or disappointment in him, he can let go of feelings like these too. You will be modeling for him a mastery of your emotions and a generosity of spirit that will make both of you feel better—and close again.

When a child's misbehavior is turned into an opportunity for him to grow and learn, forgiveness:

- Reaffirms the child's sense that at least one adult believes in him, no matter what.
- Protects or restores a child's positive feelings about himself.
- Rebuilds a child's sense that he is able to do better.
- Teaches a child to shift perspectives and to forgive himself.

Apologies

Apologies are powerful when they express recognition of the feelings of others and genuine caring about them. It's best to avoid demanding apologies prematurely, since this is likely to lead to insincere ones, or to power struggles. Apologies are not apologies if they are forced or extracted. Like reparations, they not only make the victim feel better, but they make the misbehaving child feel better too. A heartfelt apology is an important step toward not only being forgiven, but feeling forgiven too.

CHAPTER FOUR

Ways to Discipline

When faced with a child's misbehavior, parents are bound to consider ways to discipline that come from a variety of sources: one's own instincts or childhood experiences of being disciplined, the ways that other parents or teachers use that seem to work, or suggestions from books, magazines, and websites. As you make your choices, it will help to remember both your goal for discipline and the fact that your child will be learning about you and modeling on your behavior.

As you proceed through the five steps of discipline described in the last chapter, you will be looking for ways to discipline that help a child learn how she can stop herself, how she can get control of her emotions, recognize that what she did was wrong and what it means to others, and think about what will keep her from making the same mistakes again. With disciplinary strategies that allow for this kind of teaching, you will accomplish much more than stopping and punishing a particular instance of "bad" behavior. Your child will be learning to keep herself from misbehaving the next time. Don't expect this to come together all at once. This is a long-term project, and repetition and patience will be needed.

We have organized these common ways to discipline into three categories: usually worth a try, sometimes useful, and not helpful.

Usually Worth a Try

Warnings

Warnings help a child set limits on activities she may not want to give up. When you warn a child that a change is coming soon, you help her get ready for disappointment about stopping what she's doing. "In 15 minutes, we'll have to gather up our things to go home. You won't like it, and I'm sorry to make you leave your friends, but they'll be here tomorrow. For today, it will soon be time to stop." Another warning at 5 minutes, then a firm, "Now it's time. I'll help you get yourself together." The warnings have firmed up your own resolve just as they've prepared your child.

At bedtime, no child likes to give up. "One more book!" "I need a glass of water!" "I need to go to the potty!" Make clear that you will stick to two warnings, and then insist on turning out the lights. You might say, "This is your first book. After this, one more. Then lights off." After the first book, another warning: "This is the second book. Remember, it is the last one before we turn off the lights, so get yourself ready." Being wishy-washy confuses a child. Definite warnings and a firm, expected closure are reassuring.

Pros

—Teaches a child to get ready for change, models planning.
—Teaches a child to recognize her moods (for example, frustration or excitement) and to take control of them as she prepares herself for change.
—Deals with the reality that changes and transitions are hard for many children, who often are unable to handle them smoothly without an adult's help.

Cons

—Won't work if warnings are extended or not followed through on.
—May not work when a child is so deeply involved in an activity that she can't stop, or so resistant to the next activity that she won't voluntarily do it.

Silence
Silence can be a powerful form of discipline. Children are used to being told continuously what to do and what not to do. When this expectation is disrupted by silence, a child is likely to realize the serious aspect of her behavior. She will long for communication again. After the silence, little explanation may be necessary. If it is, be brief. "You know I can't tolerate that, don't you?"

Pros

—A surprising and effortless way of getting a child's attention and stopping the action.

Cons

—Can be experienced by the child as an emotional withdrawal by the parent.

—May be damaging if used frequently and without chances afterward to talk together and understand what happened.

—If the reason for silence remains a mystery, the child is bound to think that her infraction was so bad that there is no way to make up for it.

Time-Out

Time-outs include sending the child to her room, to a special chair, or to the corner.

There are many instances of misbehavior when a child is simply too excited or worked up to be able to stop herself and think about what she is doing. But this is exactly what she will need to do before any other form of discipline can be effective. The goal here is to break the momentum of out-of-control behavior.

Since the point of a time-out, whether in the child's room or elsewhere, is for her to calm herself down, it is important not to continue interacting with her while she is working on this. Contact with you may get her upset all over again, and negotiations at this point are bound to fail. You can let her know that you will be nearby and that you are ready to talk when she's calmed herself down. She needs to know that although you are leaving her to settle herself, you are not abandoning her. If it seems to be taking a long time for a child to settle down, you may need to offer some suggestions: "Would you like a cold washcloth to put on your face?" "Maybe listening to some music that you like would help?"

Time-outs can be a very helpful way of handling discipline. Children learn to expect it, to even recognize their own need for it. "I'm putting myself in a time-out, Mommy." Use it firmly. No arguments or teasing about it. Make it short. When it achieves its goal, don't wait. Go straight to the child to let her know that you love her, but not her behavior: "When you lose control, I have to do something to stop you, until you can stop yourself."

If a child refuses to go on a time-out in her room or elsewhere, it may be that a parent has not given the instruction firmly and de-cisively. Sometimes it is necessary to use a reward or punishment: "When you're done with the time-out, you can go out and play again," or "If you don't start your time-out right away, then I'll have to send your friend home." A child doesn't need to be isolated for longer than it takes for her to get herself under control, unless there is another task she needs to work on next: getting ready to apologize, for example, or thinking over how she can make repa-rations. She may, however, need to stay away from a situation that is likely to start up the whole cycle again. If this is the case, the child needs to find a different way of handling this situation, and may need your help for this.

The child's room, or chair, or corner can become a symbol for controlling herself. If she keeps popping back out before she's under control, you may need to consider putting her in her room with a gate or chain lock on the door. Then she will need both a warning and reassurance: "Since you can't stay there until you are in control, I'll have to use the gate (or chain lock) to help keep you in control until you can do it yourself. But as soon as you are OK, I'll come to get you."

A chain or gate is a last resort. Many children will never need these, and most who do should not need them often. When there is no avoiding them, a chain or gate across the door allows some communication, while being a firm symbol of containment. The child needn't feel shut away, as she would if the door were closed.

Pros

—Stops the misbehavior.

—Gives parents a chance to calm themselves, and teaches a child to pay attention to her out-of-control feelings.

—Gives a child practice in getting herself back under control. She can learn to feel proud of accomplishing this.

—Breaks a cycle of negative interactions with others (including parents or siblings) that may be contributing to the misbehavior.

—Gives the child a chance to think over what she has done, and to make plans to behave differently.

—Creates a routine, useful for future episodes, that everyone can rely on.

Cons

—The child may refuse to take the time-out or stay where she is told.

—In her room, the child may damage or break things. If these are belongings that the child values, this can be a sign of more serious difficulties in handling out-of-control feelings.

—Loses its impact if used too often. Room, Chair, or Corner?

Many children (and parents) need the comfort of a routine place for time-outs. Use it. But be ready to switch to another spot when this isn't available. Many parents find that the time-out needn't be in a lonely spot. Often, simply stopping the action and sitting quietly is enough. A childcare teacher I know once told me, "I don't believe in time-outs. The kids don't need to be sent away, or isolated. When they misbehave, I just tell them they need to go sit on the sofa. There they have to stop and think about what they've done. But they are comfortable there, and they can relax and watch the other kids. That's the best way to learn, and it always seems to be enough. Then I go over and give them a hug. We talk about what they did wrong, and how they can do better." A few weeks later, he told me that the fire department made him get rid of his sofa, which was not flame-resistant. The children were all very sad to see it go!

There may be some occasions, however, when some form of limited isolation is necessary to stop the action and settle the child. Some children—for example, hypersensitive or hyperactive ones—may really need to be removed from the action before they can calm themselves. Also, in a group of children, a child forced to sit in a corner or conspicuous chair may feel humiliated, which is neither desirable nor necessary.

Doing Something Over Again—the Right Way

This is a wonderful way for the child to regain self-control and a feeling of effectiveness. Offer (but don't push) to help her master it. You will be giving her a chance to succeed and backing up her sense that she can succeed.

Pros

—Focuses on success, not failure.
—Gives a child hope.
—Encourages a child to make reparations, and be forgiven.

—Can be applied to many situations (what a child does, what a child says).

—Children (like adults) often need a second chance in order to get something right.

Cons

—Occasionally a child may not be able or ready to get something right. Putting too much emphasis on another try can make a child feel worse. In that case, try breaking the task (for example, cleaning the child's room) into smaller steps (such as putting dirty clothes in the laundry hamper). Have the child redo only the steps that she can succeed at.

Reparations

There are many strategies that allow a child to make reparations: apologies, paying back, doing something over again—the right way. When a child can repair the damages she has done, letting her do so is a wonderful way to impress her with the extent of the damage and with the work needed to repair it. After a child has taken a toy or has stolen a piece of candy, being sure that she returns it is a critical way of handling the theft. "Of course it's embarrassing, but you will feel so much better afterward." If necessary, help her by accompanying her. But she needs to be the one who returns it, with an apology. If the item has been eaten, make the child pay for it with her own money or do chores to earn the money.

Help a child realize the meaning of her act for others. She must face her own guilt, understand the meaning of her act for her "victim," and must relive the act in the apology. Offer to help her apologize, but expect her to do it—preferably person to person. The experience will teach a child the power of words and the importance of careful communication with others.

Pros

—Helps the child recognize the consequences of her behavior.

—Helps the child learn that "crime does not pay."

—Can teach the child problem-solving skills.

— Allows the child to recognize guilty feelings and redeem herself.

Cons

—Can burden a child with guilt if the damages are exaggerated or the reparations are impossible to carry out. Returning an item to a store or friend's house can be embarrassing to both child and parents. But better the embarrassment now than when the child is older.

Forgiveness

To be forgiven is the goal of any apology or reparation. If she is to be motivated to make amends, a child needs to know that she can be forgiven, and what it feels like to be forgiven. Sometimes children dig in their heels, continue to stir up trouble, and say, "I don't care." Often they have begun to believe that they are truly "bad." These children need to be reminded that they can be forgiven. Later, they will need to learn to forgive themselves.

Pros

—Offers a child hope and gives her one of the most important incentives of all for improving behavior.

Cons

—If parents hold their power to forgive over a child like a weapon, she may not learn to become the judge of her own acts, a long-term goal of discipline.

Planning

Many misbehaviors are predictable. Many situations can be predicted to lead to trouble. Why not talk these over in advance, and plan out alternatives together? "I know it is hard for you to ride in the car for such a long time. What things can we bring to help you keep yourself busy?" "When we go to the checkout counter, I know you may be tempted to ask for candy. And you know that I won't let you have it. What would help you get yourself past the cash register without begging? We could bring a healthy snack. Or you could shut your eyes tight until we are past the candy—I'll hold your hand. What are your ideas?"

You can also help a child learn to plan to pay attention to her feelings. A child can keep track of her "escalator of trouble," and what kinds of things are likely to set her off. She can learn to tell you when she's starting to feel like she's on her way up, and how you can help.

But be prepared for troubles to break through anyway, and don't feel discouraged.

Pros

—Teaches a child to plan, and to problem-solve.
—Child and parents become a team trying to face a predictable time of trouble together.

Cons

—The child may feel that she is expected to misbehave, unless this planning is handled positively.
—Discouragement is a risk if the child and the parents expect too much from planning.

Humor

Humor is a delightful way to stop the action, help a child grab hold of her feelings, and change them. Finding something funny about a situation that's been making everybody upset is a great way to take a new perspective and find a solution. Be careful, though, not to use humor that might make an out-of-control child feel like you are laughing at her.

Humor is different from sarcasm, which never helps.

Pros

—Teaches the child a skill she'll need for the rest of her life.
—Keeps molehills from turning into mountains.

Cons

—Risks being misunderstood and experienced as humiliation.
—Can backfire if the child feels that she's the butt of the joke.

Sometimes Useful

The effectiveness of these strategies depends on the child and on the situation.

Taking Away Toys

Play is a child's work. Toys are a child's tools. Taking away a child's toys certainly will get her attention, and make her upset. A child must understand the reason for taking them away if a parent is to be respected as a model of fairness. Good reasons to take away toys include: misusing them, breaking them, using them to hurt someone, refusing to share or take turns, refusing to put toys

away after play. All of these misbehaviors are directly related to a
child's use of toys, and she can be helped to see the connection:
"If you keep trying to hit your little brother with that truck, I'll
have to take it away," or "If you are going to leave your toys all
over the floor, I'll have to put them all away in my closet. When
you get one back from me, you'll have to put that one away before
you get the next one."

When you take a child's toy away:

- Make sure there is a good reason, one that the child can
  understand.
- Be clear about how long the toy will be taken away, and exactly what the child will need to do (apologize for hitting,
  put away her other toy, etc.) in order to get her toy back.
- Don't take it away for too long: a child needs to be able
  to hold on to hope in order to face her mistake. An afternoon or a day is usually long enough for a young child. If
  you take it away for too long, she will forget you have it,
  and then the next threat of having a toy taken away may
  not mean much.

Pros

—Stops the unwanted behavior, especially if the behavior involved the toy.
—Allows for teaching.
—Allows the child to hope, to apologize or make reparations,
and to be forgiven.

Cons

—Parent may be seen as unfair, unreasonable, or coercive if
the reason for taking away the toy is not clear to the child.

—Even if this strategy is used fairly, a child may first react with anger, even a tantrum. Don't give in to it.

Don't take away a toy (such as a teddy bear) that a child is deeply attached to. This is too big a blow. The child is bound to experience this as out of proportion to any misbehavior she'd be capable of. Such a terrible loss is likely to prevent her from being able to think about anything else, let alone her misbehavior and its consequences. Instead, let her keep her beloved source of comfort so that she can use it to soothe herself as the two of you talk over what she has done and what she'll need to do to make things better. If she can cling to her teddy bear, she's more likely to be able to handle strong feelings like guilt and shame that can otherwise make it hard to face what must be faced.

Canceling Play Dates or Postponing Pleasurable Activities

Canceling play dates and postponing pleasurable activities are useful forms of discipline because they confront a child with the consequences of her behavior. A parent can explain, "I can't let you have your friend come over to play if you're not going to listen to me. I need to know that you and your friend will listen if you both are going to play here. You're going to have to play by yourself this afternoon. Then we can see if you are doing a better job of listening." Or, "We're not going to be able to go to the amusement park after a tantrum. You need to be able to keep yourself in control to go to a place like that." When these strategies are used, they should be tied to the reason. "You are so upset today that we'd better postpone your play date until you can have fun with your friend. She'll want you to come whenever we can plan it again. But you need to get hold of yourself in order to play with her. When you're ready, we'll call her again."

Make sure the child knows how the punishment is related to the misbehavior. The child also needs to know when the punishment will end and what she has to do to earn back the chance to play with another child. Otherwise, a child will feel desperate, and may not bother to try to improve her behavior.

Pros

—Helps the child understand that her own out-of-control behavior will interfere with a demanding situation such as a play date.
—When well explained, gives a child a reason for improving her behavior.

Cons

—It is not helpful to cancel a play date or fun activity as a punishment for an unrelated misbehavior. When a punishment doesn't make sense, a child is bound to question a parent's authority and will look for secret ways to get what she wants. Play dates with friends and activities with parents are important to a child, and should not be taken away often.
—Canceling plans may penalize not just your child, but also her playmate or other family members. This can create more anger at your child than her misbehavior warrants.
—Canceling plans may not be effective if they are far off. Most disciplinary strategies require that a consequence be imposed and felt by the child immediately.
—It may be difficult to make a reasonable connection between the child's misbehavior and the canceled event.

No TV or Video Games

Parents may not want to encourage certain activities that children find enjoyable, for example, watching television shows and playing video games. Yet if these are taken away as punishment, they will seem even more exciting to the child. Of course these activities should be limited anyway (no more than an hour a day of television). Take away the allowed TV or video game time only when such activities are directly related to the problem. "If you can't turn off the TV when your show is over, then the TV will stay off tomorrow." Be sure to stick to consequences like these, especially when they are so far off. A parent can remind a child, "Remember yesterday how hard it was for you to turn the TV off when it was time? I had to tell you there would be no TV today, and there won't be. Try to remember tomorrow, when your show is done, that the TV needs to be turned off—without fussing."

Pros

—Can stop misbehavior, and may also prevent more misbehavior.

—The child can learn about the consequences of her behavior.

—The child can appreciate that some fun activities are privileges to be earned instead of taken for granted.

Cons

—May make TV and video games even more alluring.

—Restricting TV or video games as a punishment may become confused with the family's standard limits on these.

Ignoring Misbehavior

Ignoring minor misbehavior when there are other more important issues to be addressed is critical. A child who is constantly reprimanded for one incident after another is a child who will stop listening. Ignoring misbehavior may be necessary in order to pick your battles. However, ignoring misbehavior is a mistake if the misbehavior is serious, or if the child has already been warned about or punished for it.

Pros

—Allows a parent to select important areas for discipline.
—The child is more likely to pay attention to disciplinary strategies when they are not overused.
—Discourages minor irritating misbehavior that is designed to get a parent's attention.

Cons

—The child may be confused about why some of her misdeeds are not being responded to.

Leaving the Scene

Sometimes a parent's presence just seems to make things worse. This can happen when a child is angry about a rule and blames having to follow it on the parent. Then the sight of the parent just inflames her more. If the child can safely be left alone at this point, a parent's departure may help the child focus on the rule, or on what needs to be done, rather than on the parent's role in telling her about it. "You know you have to clean your room now, and I know you're not happy about it. But it needs to be done, and I know you can do it. I'll check back a little later to see how you're doing." This gives the child a chance to settle herself and think about what she's done wrong, or what she can do to improve the situation. The next conversation you have together is likely to be more constructive. Disengaging from a struggle in which the important point has been lost is often helpful.

Whenever a parent leaves the scene, it is essential that the child understands that she is not being rejected or abandoned. It is not possible to learn under that kind of stress. Let her know it's the behavior you don't like, not the child herself. Share with her your hope that she'll be able to control herself in the future.

Pros

—Stops the struggle.

—Turns the work of calming down and problem solving over to the child. This can be done in a way that makes the child feel respected.

Cons

—May be experienced as a rejection.

—Won't work if the child needs a parent's help to settle herself down.

—Leaving the child to accomplish something on her own without being certain that she can is not helpful.

Extra Chores

For an older child, this may be helpful. But the extra chores should be directly related to the child's misbehavior. For example, if a child who is old enough to know better intentionally damages an expensive object, a parent might require that she do some extra work around the house to help make up for it and "pay off the debt."

Pros

—Gives the child a chance to make reparations and be forgiven. She's unlikely to forget what she will have learned.

—When chores are done, a parent has the opportunity to forgive and praise the child.

Cons

—Extra chores as punishment for unrelated troublemaking are a mistake. As soon as helping around the house is turned into a punishment for "bad" behavior, no child will ever feel good again about helping out. More protests against chores than ever will be the likely result.

—Extra chores as a punishment can also backfire by presenting opportunities for a rebellious child to mess up the chore or to ignore it. Then the purpose of the discipline is lost in the power struggle that is likely to ensue.

Docked Allowance

If the allowance is meaningful to the child, docking a part of it may be a way of impressing her with the seriousness of her misbehavior. But if a child is to be disciplined—for example, for being rude and disrespectful to an adult or for hurting another child's feelings—taking an allowance away sends a confusing message. Not all mistakes or misbehaviors can be corrected with money.

Sometimes, though, holding back on an allowance does make sense: for example, to pay for an object that a child broke on purpose, or for something that was lost because it was not properly put away. An allowance can also be withdrawn when a child fails to carry out one of her usual household duties. In any case, be sure that the financial repayment is appropriate to the child's age, and to what she's done.

Pros

—Helps a child to feel the effect of her behavior.
—Gives the child a chance to make up for what she's done.

Cons

—Doesn't stop the behavior, since this consequence occurs after the fact, though it may help prevent further similar problems.
—Doesn't work for children who don't receive allowances.
—When used as punishment for failure to do chores, a child may have the impression that she is hired help, rather than seeing that helping out with chores is an expected part of belonging to a family.

Not Helpful

Spanking

Using physical punishment needs to be avoided as much as possible today. I was switched whenever I "deserved" it when I was little, but I don't remember anything I learned from it, except to hide the switch from my parents. Hitting a child is not respectful. It shows that you are bigger than she is (which won't last) and it tells her that violence is the way to settle issues. In our present violent society, I can't recommend this as a way of helping a child learn to control herself.

I would avoid using force as a way to control a child. The goal of discipline is to teach the child how to control herself. Force won't lead to that. These days we can no longer afford to take the "spare the rod, spoil the child" dictum so literally. It is time we took it to mean "spare discipline, spoil the child"—a challenging but essential warning for every parent.

Pros

—May stop the unwanted behavior, for the moment, and as long as the parent is present.

Cons

—Sends the child the wrong message: that it is okay to hit, to physically hurt, and to use force against someone who is smaller and less powerful.
—Does not teach. The child is likely to focus on her hurt and anger, rather than on learning about what she did wrong.
—May discredit the parent as a model and teacher (see also "Physical Punishment" on page 39 in chapter 2).

Shame and Humiliation

Never humiliate a child. A child's own guilt and realization of what she's done is so much more important. When parents use shame and humiliation to control a child's behavior, the child is likely to feel anger, desperation, and hopelessness. As a result, the child will need to deny and defend, rather than acknowledge what she has done wrong.

Pros

—May stop the behavior, temporarily.

Cons

—Does not teach.

—May damage the child's self-esteem.

—May damage the child–parent relationship.

Soap Mouthwash

This is another ineffective measure. Whenever I said a dirty word, my mouth was washed with soap. It produced a horrid taste, but even worse, it was insulting. I knew that it wouldn't clean up my speech. I knew it was out-of-control behavior on my mother's part. I just saved up the dirty words for my friends, and my brother—in private. I learned nothing, except to avoid letting my mother hear me swear.

Pros

—None. By the time you get to the bar of soap, the behavior has already stopped.

Cons

—Coercion is required, which creates resentment, rather than willingness to be corrected, in the child.

—Unhealthy and sends a confusing message to the child about what is safe to eat.

—Parent's usual role of feeding a child is violated, which may be more disturbing to the child than the parent suspects.

Comparing One Child to Another

If the other child is a sibling or good friend, negative comparisons are bound to damage their relationships. A child can certainly model on someone she looks up to. But she's bound to fail if she tries to be like someone who she's been told she doesn't measure up to.

Pros

—A child may learn from an admired friend, especially if parents refrain from making unfavorable comparisons.

Cons

—Interferes with the child's relationships.
—Damages self-esteem.
—Can make a child feel hopeless, and does not encourage improvement.
—The wounded child may decide not to care, and behave even worse.

Withholding Food or Using It as a Reward

Parents may be tempted to withhold dessert or a favorite food as punishment, or to offer a special treat as a reward. But since parents feed a child from the beginning of life, uncondition-ally, food becomes a symbol of a parent's love. A punishment should not withdraw love, nor should it take away food. A re-ward should not offer extra love—or food. These are things that we wish all children could know they will have enough of, no matter what.

Meals are special times for parents and children to be together, relax, and enjoy each other. If battles emerge at mealtime, it is best not to try to settle them with punishments or rewards involving food. Keep food and mealtimes as free of negative associations as possible so that children will continue to enjoy nourishing them-selves and spending time with their families.

In battles over food, a child will inevitably win. Parents will do best to accept this. Healthy eating habits depend on positive associations with food and mealtimes. Sometimes parents try to use food to control a child's behavior: "If you'll eat this, you can have dessert." Then eating becomes a bargaining process. Instead of enjoying a meal as a pleasurable time for family communication, the child feels manipulated. If she has spirit, she'll wait until she is no longer under pressure, and find something to eat—which may be junk food.

Desserts should not be used as a reward, but as a part of the meal that is shared.

Pros

—May temporarily have the desired effect on immediate behavior.

Cons

—This is not a safe place for a parent–child battleground.
—Healthy eating habits can be disturbed by turning food into a punishment, or a reward.
—Withheld desserts or sweets become more desirable.

Early Bedtimes and Extra Naps

Naps and bedtimes require a child to separate from parents and the rest of the world. These are already challenging times for a child, and resistance is likely. Turning naps or bedtimes into a punishment will only make them less appealing, and make the child resist them even more. Naps and bedtimes need positive associations, not negative ones.

Even if "You'll go to bed early" is used as a threat that a parent has no intention of enforcing, the association of bedtime with punishment has still been made. Bedtime should be a time of warm communication, of reading, singing, lying close to each other, feeling safe and protected, feeling loved. All of these are at stake when going to bed is used as punishment.

If a child has been misbehaving because she is overtired, then an early bedtime makes sense—not as a punishment, but as a way to help.

Pros

—May temporarily stop misbehavior.

Cons

—Can make a child's bedtime struggles worse.
—Can be difficult to enforce.

Withdrawing Affection and Threatening Abandonment

These are the most devastating and feared punishments that a child can endure. Their long-term effects on the child are serious, and can lead to fearfulness, insecurity, and poor self-esteem.

Pros

—May stop behavior temporarily.

Cons

—Does not teach.
—May damage child–parent relationship.
—A child who does not feel loved may become unable to love.
—Without love, resentment and hatred can take hold in a child and lead to more serious behavioral problems.

As we said earlier, a child needs to know that her relationships with her parents will always withstand her "bad" behavior. Any threat to that relationship prevents the child from hearing the lesson at hand, and she may misbehave on purpose, needing to test out whether her behavior might drive her parents away.

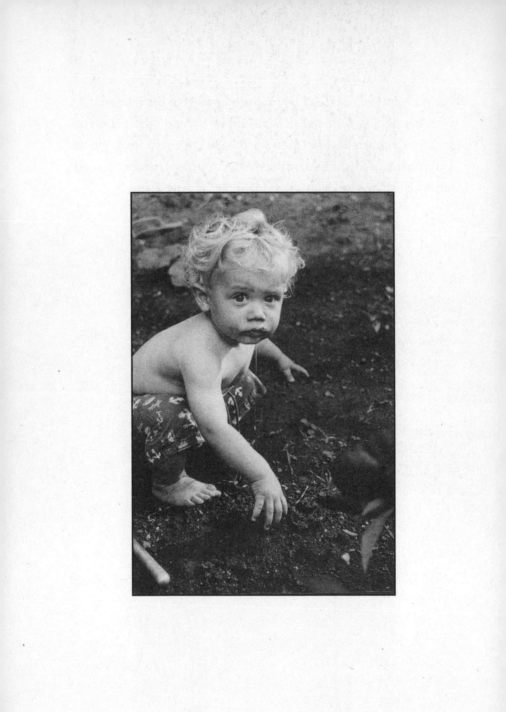

CHAPTER FIVE

Common Behavior Problems

Always Looking for Attention

No one likes a child who is always looking for attention. Yet, of course, every child needs attention. What can a parent do when a child's attention seeking becomes disruptive and, worse still, turns everyone against him? First of all, be sure to give him regular, reliable, uninterrupted times with you that are just for him—10 minutes to cuddle when you get home at the end of the day, a bedtime story every night, waffle making together on Sunday morning. Don't make these a reward for troublesome attention seeking, but make them his, before he starts looking for your attention. When he wants attention but can't have it, remind him of the special times he knows he can count on. You are helping him to learn to delay gratification. Some of life's most important rewards require patience.

When disruptive attention seeking begins, it is important not to reinforce it. A parent can respond in a low-key and neutral tone that makes it clear such behavior will not be rewarded: "If you need me for something, that's not the way to ask. You know how." When the child intensifies his demanding behavior, a similarly calm and clear response can help: "You need to understand that no matter how many more times you ask, I am not going to be able to help you just now." It is also important to direct the child to alternative behaviors, other solutions: "I have to finish what I'm doing right now, but in 15 minutes I should be done, and then I'll come help you. In the meantime, you'll have a lot more fun playing with your blocks or coloring than you will just hanging around waiting for me."

Often a child who seems to seek attention constantly has trouble being alone. It is not a parent's job to provide constant companionship and entertainment, but to help the child learn to entertain himself. (TV and video games are tempting solutions, but they don't leave enough up to the child.) You may have to start by helping him see that he is feeling lonely or bored, or that he just doesn't know what to do with himself. He needs to learn to handle these feelings. You can direct the attention he does get from you in these moments to helping him learn how. Before suggesting things he can do, ask him to think about what would make him feel better, about what he would like to do. Eventually he will learn to ask himself these questions, and to find his own answers.

Begging and Whining

A child who repeatedly whines is a child who has found this to be an effective form of communication. Every time a parent responds to whining with even a "yes" or a "no" to the demand, instead of a simple "Stop whining," the child learns that whining can work. When a child whines or fusses, parents should not respond to what the child is saying, but to how the child is saying it. A child who whines for "one more climb up the slide" can be told firmly, "Whining won't get you anything," or "When you whine I won't listen," or "I can't even think about what you're asking unless you can ask without whining." It is, of course, important to live up to statements like these. If the child then changes his tone of voice, his request should be honored, if it is a reasonable one. If it is not, a parent can praise the child for changing his tone, point out to him that now he has been heard, and then explain why his request cannot be granted.

Sometimes there are other reasons for whining. Children who are stressed by a new challenge in their own development may fuss and whine. So will children under other kinds of pressure—a move, a new school, parents who aren't getting along. Even so, children need parents to help them see the effect of whining on others. "When you whine like that, no one wants to listen." Parents can help children see that whining won't help them get what they need by being sure not to give in to it. Other ways of talking that are more likely to be taken seriously can be suggested or modeled. Parents can respond to the pressures a child is feeling without responding to whining.

Begging is similar. A child is bound to beg when he knows it's worked before. When parents waver, a child senses that he may have a chance—if not this time, then the next. When the child's demand sets one parent against the other ("It won't hurt him to have one more. Why do you have to be so rigid?"), then begging may even become its own reward!

When the answer is "no," it must be perfectly clear, and consistent from one time to the next. Sometimes, though, parents may want to be able to buy a special treat at the store on some occasions, and not at others. Won't the child learn that sometimes begging does pay off? Not if the parent stays in control: "If you beg for something at the store, you can be sure you will not be allowed to have it. If you can ask politely, then I'll decide whether you can or not. But once I've said no, that's it, and I expect you to accept it." If the child protests, a parent may need to add, "We'd both hate for you to make a big fuss over this. But either way, no candy this time." A child will be relieved to know that a parent can withstand her distress, and that rules can too.

Young children will sometimes beg because they truly cannot imagine how they'll withstand the disappointment of living without the candy or toy that has caught their attention at the moment. Here, too, a clear and consistent "no" is essential. But more may be needed when a child is still having trouble handling overwhelming feelings—of anger, frustration, disappointment.

Sometimes it's helpful to warn the child that he'll need to brace himself before he actually hears the bad news: "You know sometimes you get very upset when you can't have what you want. So you may need to get yourself ready." Then sympathizing with his feelings will help him to see that you are still on his side, even though you can't let him have what he wants right now: "I can see how disappointed you'll be if you can't have it." Then give him the reason for your refusal: "But you know you can't get a new toy every time we come to the store. So we're not going to get one this time." When he starts to beg and plead, you can say: "No matter what you say, you need to know that we're not getting that toy. But I hate to see you feeling so miserable, and I'd like to try to help you make yourself feel better. But not by getting that toy. Let's think about other things we can do to have fun."

Biting—and Hitting, Kicking, and Scratching

Early in the second year, a baby starts to bite. One pediatrician we know says, "For toddlers, a kiss and a bite are not very far apart." When he bites his parent, he is likely to be so startled that he cries out too.

Two 2-year-olds fight over a toy. They pull and push and claw at each other's fingers to gain possession. Finally, without thinking, one lunges toward the other, grabs an arm with both of his hands. In a flash, he sinks his teeth into the other child's flesh. Both children dissolve into blood-curdling shrieks and a pool of tears.

When one child bites another, the whole neighborhood goes crazy. "He's a biter! I can't let my child play with him." Biting, hitting, kicking, and scratching start out as reactions to being excited, or overloaded. The child builds up to a peak, then he bites or hits or kicks or scratches. Everyone overreacts. The child repeats it, not out of anger or aggression, but out of high tension. With any of this normal-in-the-beginning behavior, trouble arises when adults around the child enlarge on its meaning: "He's an aggressive 2-year-old. Steer clear." When parents and teachers react excitedly, the child may quickly learn to use biting as a way of getting quick, reliable attention, and even as a weapon. At a loss for more winning behaviors, he may bite again. Very soon he will be labeled and deserted, making biting and other aggressive behaviors more likely. But if adults can react more calmly, biting will lose its value, and is very likely to stop.

When a toddler bites a parent, the parents often ask, "Should I bite him back?" Our response is: Absolutely not. You don't want to be on her level of development, do you? Just put the child down calmly and walk away, saying, "I don't like that." But don't make a big deal of it. When a child bites another child, of course the child who has been hurt needs protection and comfort. But so does the child who has attacked—protection from his own impulses, and the security that will allow him to face his responsibility. A child who hurts another must face what he has done, but punishment that floods him with guilt can overwhelm him. In that case, he'll need to deny what he's done, rather than learn from it. You can make the limit clear while also offering the child a chance to redeem himself and to be forgiven. He can also learn a lesson for the next time. "Of course you feel awful that you made your friend cry. You wanted that toy so badly. But now you know how badly you feel when you hurt a friend to get what you want. Let me give you a hug, and then we can go over to him so you can say you're sorry."

At 2 years of age, a child needs to learn to understand and care about others, though this is of course a lifelong process. When he hurts someone else, he feels threatened too. Until he can stop himself, he will be grateful to know that adult limit setting will keep him from hurting others, and himself. For now, that responsibility is too great for the child to bear alone.

I used to keep a list of toddlers in my pediatric office so parents could get them together for play dates. But I needed to break down the list into biters, hitters, scratchers, or kickers. Then parents could match their toddler with a fitting companion. When one child bit his peer, the other biter bit back. Each of them howled and looked at each other as if to say, "That hurt! Why did you do it?" and they didn't bite each other again.

Unless biting or kicking or other such behavior lasts into the third or fourth year, it rarely needs to be taken seriously. If it does continue, you may need to be concerned about the child's reason for needing this aggressive, upsetting behavior. If the older child resorts to this behavior frequently, you will need to address the underlying reasons, as well as the symptoms, by getting help from your pediatrician or a child psychologist or psychiatrist. There can be many causes for this disturbing behavior—for example, frustration due to delayed development of language or social skills, or exposure to violence.

Bullying

A bully is likely to be an insecure child. By bullying a weaker or smaller child, a child may make himself feel more secure. A bully is most likely to choose a child who is clearly vulnerable, and who suffers visibly when bullied. This, of course, adds fuel to the flame. As the bullying child becomes more excited, he may turn from teasing to pushing or hitting. Both children are frightened.

As with other aggression between children, each child needs your comfort. The bullied child needs to be protected, and encouraged to defend himself. Perhaps he could say, "You sound weird when you tease like that. Have you ever heard yourself?" Few bullies will dare to continue if the victim does not act like one and can begin to stand up for himself. A child who has been a victim of bullying may feel better if he can learn a martial art for self-defense. If he knows he can fight back, he may never need to use these new skills. He will seem more confident, and be a less likely target for a bully's taunts.

Bullies sniff out the vulnerable child. A weaker child threatens them because they are reminded of their own weaknesses. This is why a bully needs your help even more. His self-confidence is fragile. His self-esteem can be shattered by retaliation. Pick him up to hold him and rock him. "No one likes to be bullied. I know you want friends, and you want them to like you, but they won't if you do that. Let's try to find you a friend who will be like you, and can tease you back. You'll have fun and both learn how to make friends without bullying. You'll be proud." Watch for situations in which a child who bullies is secure, and comment on them. Try to understand why he feels so insecure. Does he feel embarrassed about having failed to develop certain skills? Is there no adult to look up to and identify with, whom he knows admires him? Perhaps he has not yet learned how to make a bid for another child's friendship. Perhaps his abilities to interact with peers, to negotiate and make compromises, to control his temper are too limited for him to hold on to friends. Perhaps he has been threatened himself, and now tries to reassure himself that he is too tough to be in danger. A child with difficulties in any of these areas can generally overcome them with an adult's understanding and help.

Cheating

Sooner or later, any child will cheat. He may be playing a game that is too advanced for him. He may need more chances to play games that he can win. A child who cheats may not yet fully understand the rules. Or he may not be able to hold back on his impulse to win at all costs.

Often, a child who cheats is saying: "I can't bear the thought of losing." A child who invests all the self-esteem he's got in a single game is desperate, and can't afford to lose. His belief in his own value is fragile, and games seem like a risky opportunity to strengthen it. A child's self-esteem can become more fragile as he matures enough to become aware of his limitations, how small he really is, and how much he relies on his parents. When he is disciplined for cheating, he is likely to add to his misdeeds by lying: "I did NOT take two cards!"

A parent's discipline can help him face up to his cheating if his self-esteem is protected. It can also help him learn to control his impulses: "I know you wanted to win this game very badly. And you were playing so well! But you and I both know you were cheating. I can understand why you cheated, but I can't accept it. Cheating isn't anything that either you or I can feel good about. You know that you can't really feel proud of winning if you have to cheat."

Even if he is not ready to stop cheating, it is important to make sure he understands how much more satisfied he will feel when he can win without cheating. To help him with this, be sure to play plenty of games with him that he can win. When he beats you, model how to be a "good loser" with your own behavior.

Most children who cheat at 5 or 6 years of age will eventually stop. As children get older, it becomes easier for them to wait for the pleasure of really winning without cheating. As they become more skilled, it is easier for them to take pleasure in just playing the game, and easier for them to lose without feeling bad about themselves.

Defiance

When your child is defiant, he is "in your face." There isn't any guessing about what he's up to. "No, I won't," "Make me," and

"I'd like to see you try" are commonly heard when a child is defying a parent.

Children often need to defy their parents—even when they know their defiance is wrong. Sometimes, defiance is a child's way of trying to feel powerful, and independent. Other children are defiant when they feel too powerful, when their own power frightens them. Then they are hungry for limits.

Defiance may serve as a test to see whether parents really mean what they say. Then when the initial defiance creates increasing anger in parents, a child may try to use more defiance to fend off his parents.

Defiance is very difficult for parents to deal with. They may overreact for a number of reasons:

- The defiance makes them feel not only angry but confused.
- They may be overreacting because their frustration with the misbehavior has been building for awhile.
- The defiance makes them question their own role: "Was I right to make this demand?"
- The defiance can force parents to take a win-or-lose position, which is unnerving and risky.
- They may be thinking ahead, picturing their child as a defiant adolescent, when their win-or-lose position may really matter.

When parents can understand their own reactions—and overreactions—and get themselves under control, they will then be more able to assess their own position, and their child's, and respond effectively.

The first step is to reevaluate your demand. Is it really that important? Then reevaluate the child's defiance. How outrageous is it? Is there any important message in the child's refusal that needs to be understood and respected?

If you decide that your demand wasn't important enough to enforce, retire gracefully and gather the benefits for a more important demand. "I like your spirit. When you question me, it makes me wonder, 'Is it worth it?' This time I think you are right. It's not that important. But when it is, I will expect you to live up to my request."

If your demand is important enough to stick to, try to stay calm but firm. Get your child's attention. Look him in the eyes. Gently put a finger underneath his chin or a hand on his shoulder if you need to. Repeat the demand, and let him know that this is not something he has a choice about. He will need to do what you ask even though you understand he does not want to. Staying calm is important so that you and he can both focus on what he needs to do. Sometimes anger can be a distraction, taking on a life of its own.

Let the child know what the consequences will be. Start with one reminder about whatever reward there might be for doing what he has been told. Pick a reward that is reasonable and closely related to the task you are asking him to do. "When you've finished cleaning your room, then we can hang up the new picture." Rewards usually work better than punishments. But as soon as he has understood your offer, it is time to stop the discussion.

If he does not respond to a reward right away, it is time to let him know what the negative consequences of his behavior will be. Pick a consequence that is reasonable, closely related to the task he's been asked to do, and simple to enforce. "If you don't start cleaning your room right away, I'll have to pick your things up off the floor and lock them in my closet until you are ready to put them away."

The most important thing about a consequence, positive or negative, is to carry it out—immediately. Let him know: "I've told you to clean your room once. I've told you what will happen if you do, and if you don't. I am now telling you for the last time that you need to clean your room. If you don't start now, then I'll have to do exactly what I said I'd do." If he still refuses, you must proceed with the negative consequence immediately, without hesitation. At this point, do not respond to any more pleas or negotiations. "It's too late now. You had your chance. Maybe you'll be able to remember that I mean what I say the next time we have a discussion like this." It's helpful to some children to know in advance what your pattern is. Soon they will know that whenever they refuse to do what you ask of them, they will have one warning, one reminder, and then the consequence.

Disobedience

A child may attempt to hide disobedient behavior, or he may flaunt it (see "Defiance," just above). Often, a small child disobeys openly, to find out what parents mean, and if they really mean it. Testing parents starts in the first year. When a seated child drops food or a toy over his high chair to see whether a parent will pick it up for him, he knows at some level that he is testing the system: "How many times can I get away with this?" A parent makes it into a game. The child is no longer sure when it is okay to throw food, and when it is not. He continues until the parent is clear: "That's enough," or "No more food," or removes him from the high chair to change the subject and clearly end the game.

At some point, dropping food on the floor is no longer accepted as a game. As a child gets older, some rules change. It can be hard for the child to keep up with the changes, and to adjust to them. Disobedience may occur when a child does not know, or is not sure about, a rule. But it also can occur when a child does know the rule, but can't bear the frustration he feels when he gives in to it.

When facing disobedience, a parent will do well to step back, pause, and:

- Stay calm and in control. Your child learns to handle his frustration by watching you.
- Evaluate the child's motive in disobeying you.
- Ask him if he knows what the rule or expectation is. Make sure he understands that the rule does apply to the current situation.
- If he truly doesn't, then this is an opportunity for learning. If he seems genuinely surprised to find out he has done something wrong, and interested in doing better the next time, negative consequences may not be necessary. Still, you will both feel better if there is a chance for him to make up for what he's done.
- Use your behavior as well as your comments to let the child know that he has been disobedient. In a calm, low voice (this will catch his attention more quickly than an out-of-control voice), say: "You simply cannot do this. I will need to stop you until you can stop yourself." This kind of statement will be useful at any age.
- If it's necessary to go further, then you can institute disciplinary tactics—a time-out, isolation, taking away

privileges, and so on. But for a less important incident, it may be enough to let him know that you are aware of his disobedient behavior and that you expect better behavior from him. There will be more-serious episodes of disobedience for which you will want to save discipline.

Make sure your child learns something from your discipline. If your child knows that what he did was wrong, why did he do it? Out of anger? To get your attention? Because he just couldn't resist the temptation? None of these will excuse his behavior, but understanding his motivation will help you decide on an effective response. If a child has acted out of anger, he will still need to face the consequences of his behavior and to make reparations. But he will also need a chance to understand what he is angry about, and to make sure that those who care about him do too. A child who disobeys to get attention needs a response that does not involve more attention, in order to avoid reinforcing his disobedience. But he will also need attention at other times, when he is not disobeying. A child who disobeys because he just can't resist will also need to face the consequences of his behavior, and to try to make up for what he has done. But he should also have help in learning about his impulses, and how to control them. "The next time you really want to take something that isn't yours, you'll need to try to stop yourself and to remember what happened this time."

Lying

Younger children may actually believe their own lies. Others may waver—sometimes able to face the unreality of a lie, sometimes needing to believe in it. But there are certainly many times when a child who lies knows that he's done something wrong. Then he lies because he can't face what he's done, or because he hopes to avoid the consequences.

When a child lies about something he knows he's done wrong, there is a positive side. He knows the difference between right and wrong. Why not give him credit for this understanding? He'll be more likely to listen when you help him to see that lying won't make what he's done wrong right.

Learning to be honest is a long-term process. Learning that lying can't change reality is an important step toward honesty. Modeling on parents who value honesty is another.

Lying is common in young children. They are struggling to accept a world that can't always be the way they'd like it to be. Lying lets children make the world into what they want it to be— until the truth must be faced. They are bound to take things that don't belong to them, or do things that they know they shouldn't and then deny that they've done anything wrong. They lie when it is just too hard to hold back on their longings. For example, the longing to be "just like Daddy" is so hard to resist. A very young boy can be expected to try out his father's clothes or desk when he is out of sight. If a father asks, "Who made a mess of my clothes?" a small child may lie openly, unable to create a convincing cover-up: "The cat did." What can a parent do?

First, a parent can accept the child's wish, even though the lying is unacceptable. A parent might say, "We both know that what you said is not true. I can understand your wanting to play with my things, but I can't be happy about your lying. You don't need to. I can stand the truth, and so can you." A calm response like this one makes it unnecessary for a child to lie.

An older child will lie more convincingly. This is more infuri-
ating for parents, and more concerning. Parents are bound to feel
angry when their child tries to trick them—especially if the child
momentarily succeeds. When a child's lies are more crafty, more
difficult to see through, parents will worry whether these new
skills are going to become a part of the child's personality. And
they may begin to wonder how they can trust their child.

When a child's lying becomes skillful and continues, it is time
to ask why the child is still struggling to accept the limits to what he
wants. It is time to ask why he feels he must lie so carefully. A child
who often lies to cover up what he has done will need more help
learning to live with the frustration of the world being the way it is.

First, he will need to know that his wishes—even those that
can't be lived out—can be understood and accepted. If he knows
he can let his parents know his wishes without being reproached
or belittled, if he can count on his parents to help him bear the
feelings that go with wishes that cannot be satisfied, then perhaps
he will not need to lie. If, on the other hand, parents respond to a
lie by criticizing both the lie and the wish behind it, then the child
may continue to feel that he needs to justify his wish, and will pay
little attention to concerns about his lying.

If parents overwhelm a child with guilt about lying, the child
may need to protect himself by convincing himself that his lie was
true, that he never really lied. It's easy to see how this can set up
a pattern of repeated lies.

It is, of course, important for parents to be clear that lying
cannot be accepted. But ultimately the child will stop lying because he has no need to, and because he has learned to criticize
himself for such behavior. If parents are too critical, he will need to
defend himself too much to be able to examine his own behavior.

When an older child lies, it is important to assure him: "I love you, but I don't like to hear you lie." Then the parent can help the child understand his reason for the lying: "I don't understand why you said that. Do you? Sometimes people tell lies when they're having trouble facing the truth." A child should know that it's never too late to make up for a lie. "Tell your teacher the truth. Even tell her why you lied—because you were so scared. She will be proud of you for telling her. I will too, and you will be proud of yourself."

If the lying continues, professional help may be needed to help sort out the reasons why the child feels it is necessary to lie.

Power Struggles

Children over 3 years of age need to establish themselves from time to time by creating a power struggle. Sometimes these struggles appear to come out of the blue. But all too often, they are predictable and occur with every demand. Temper tantrums may have waned, but power struggles may arise in their place.

When you as a parent feel yourself getting locked into such a struggle, realize that you are descending to the child's level. Can you win? Probably, by getting angry enough and establishing the fact that you are bigger and in control. Can you achieve your goal another way? Yes—by walking away until the child subsides. Then, without discussion, proceed with whatever you'd asked him to do. If he fights back again, walk away. Ignoring a child is a powerful punishment and should not be misused. When a parent walks away, it should be clear that the parent is saying, "I'll be back when you've calmed yourself down," not "I'm abandoning you because you're bad." If it's not an important struggle, forget it and save up for more important ones. If it is important, make it definite to him that there is no choice. Either he complies, or you will have to impose a consequence to help him understand the importance of your demand. By now, you and he will have recognized that the testing of power can no longer be tolerated.

Running Away

When I was a child, my grandmother lived a few blocks from us. Whenever I wanted to punish my parents for having scolded or disciplined me, I "ran away" to my grandmother's house. I pictured them suffering as I stormed off. "He's gone. We've lost him. Was it that important for us to be so mean to him?" From a distance, I enjoyed their suffering. Of course, they knew where I was, so my retaliation didn't really work. But in my mind, it did.

The meaning of running away depends on the age of a child, how the child goes about running away, and where the child actually goes. Many young children may occasionally announce that they are running away when they've been scolded, punished, or humiliated, or when they feel that their bids for attention have not been heeded. Often these announcements are made dramatically, to see if anyone seems to care. Then the child may stomp off to his room to pack a bag with a few precious belongings. He may, in fact, change his mind before he leaves his room. Or he may dawdle down the stairs toward the front door, hoping that a parent will stop him, perhaps again announcing that he is *really* leaving, and never coming back. Slamming the front door so that everyone at home can hear, he'll trudge down the front steps, looking back to see if anyone has come yet to stop him. If not, he may sit down near his house, by the house next door, or, if he is really upset, walk to a friend's house, if there is one nearby.

A young child who "runs away" like this is looking for reassurance—after a battle with his parents—that he is wanted, that he is cared for. He may also be trying to feel "big and strong," instead of small and helpless. There is something angry about running away too: "If you don't care about me, then I don't need you either," he may seem to be saying.

Of course a parent needs to keep a close eye on the child. If a parent is able to see him the whole time, and if it is perfectly safe for him to go where the parent can see him going, then he may benefit from this time to "cool off" and find that he can pull himself together on his own. If he doesn't return soon, a parent should retrieve him and reassure him that he is loved—no matter what. This is not a time for a parent to sink to the child's level. Take his feelings seriously, rather than belittling them, especially if he's just been behaving dramatically. Otherwise, he is likely to become even more dramatic. Of course, if he can't be carefully watched, or if it isn't safe for him to be alone, then he must be retrieved right away.

A young child who suddenly bolts out the door—impulsively, in anger, or in distress—must be chased and "captured" immediately, since clearly this child's behavior can't be predicted and may be dangerous. A young child who has been unhappy for a prolonged period, or is stressed by difficult life events—such as a death or other loss, bullying at school, a traumatic event—must also be held back from running away. A child like this may be trying to rejoin a lost loved one or to escape a truly unbearable situation—at any cost. Older children who run away may no longer be playing out fantasies, and may have a more desperate sense of what they must escape.

In any of these situations, the first job, after quickly retrieving the child, is to comfort him and help him settle himself. The next step is to make sure that the child knows that those who care for him still do. You will feel his body relax and sink into yours as you hold him. Then, when he is ready, give him a chance to understand what is troubling him. Finally, think together about what solutions, other than running away, might be worth trying. But children who run away impulsively, who are old enough to run too far to be found easily, who have suffered losses or traumas, or who are under stress may be crying out for more than reassurance that they are loved. They may also need the help of a mental health professional.

In our country today, the safety of a child who is by himself can no longer be counted on. Running away has become a serious situation. It cannot be tolerated as a way for a child to retaliate, even for a brief period. Both parent and child must understand this in today's more dangerous world.

Separation Problems

Many young children hate the separation of being left at childcare or school. They are likely to protest in the form of a temper tantrum. The tantrum can go on and on, as long as you are in sight. Whenever you stand up to leave, the child will start all over again. The parent is torn: "How can I leave him in this terrible state? I hate to leave him anyway, and he's in no condition to manage." Some teachers may urge you to "just leave," saying that then he will calm down. They are right. The target of the tantrum is you.

To avoid such a problem, always plan to stay with the child for the first days at a new school. Prepare him for separating from you before you leave the house. Take his favorite stuffed animal or special blanket along so he can cling to it when you leave. Tell him you'll stay a definite amount of time, then you'll have to leave—but you'll be back. Remind him that you always come back. Connect him with his teacher when you first arrive. Look at the clock together, then leave as planned. Leave him with a friend, if possible, or the teacher. Reassure him that you know the teacher will take good care of him. He counts on you to make judgments like this, and will be sensitive to any doubts you harbor.

A sensitive teacher might play a hiding game with the child: "Look at the ball go under the couch. When it's underneath we can't see it anymore. But we know it's still there. Go get it! See, it's always there. Even when you can't see it. Just like Mommy."

To deal with your own feelings about separation, hide outside the classroom to see how long he stays upset. You may be surprised how quickly he adjusts. You might also keep a diary so you can remind yourself as it gets better.

When you return, remind your child that you promised you would be back. Reassure him that you will not break the promises you make when you drop him off at school tomorrow.

At the end of the day, any child can fall apart just as the parent arrives. A temper tantrum may occur then. Someone in the childcare center or school is likely to say, "He's been great all day—with us." But rarely will anyone say, "Your child has missed you all day and tried so hard to be a 'big boy' until you came back! Now he knows he's safe enough to let everyone know how hard it has been to spend all day without you." Your own guilty feelings about being away can be overwhelming. It may be painful to you to hear his normal, healthy protest. You may even want to make him hush. Don't.

However loud the protest, gather him up and hug him tightly. "I missed you all day too. Now we can be together again." If your child ignores you or refuses to leave with you, this is all part of his protest, so don't take it to mean he hasn't missed you. Hug him close.

Sibling Rivalry

Whenever there is more than one child in a family, sibling rivalry is unavoidable. But rivalry and caring are two sides of the same coin. One is not likely to happen without the other. Caring about each other springs from learning about each other, and this comes from the inevitable squabbles of siblings. Each child learns so much from the fighting and competition. Compassion, caring, protection of one by the other will come when they tangle with siblings and peers. When there is only one child in a family, the child must find other ways to learn how to struggle, to compete, and to care about other children.

Parents are likely to take it too seriously. "Why do they always fight? Won't they ever learn to care about each other? Whose side do I take? When I get involved, it gets worse." Of course it does. Much of the fighting is aimed at the concerned parent, as each child tests out the question, "Are we both loved just the same?" Stay out of their struggles as much as you can. How can you be sure of who is to blame? You'll never be able to know who is responsible.

How to respond to siblings' struggles:

1. Walk in calmly and survey the situation.
2. If there has been no bloodshed, no sign that a child has been physically hurt, and there are no dangerous objects

around, a parent can say: "This is your battle, not mine. Let me know when you are through and I'll come back." You'll be surprised at how little it will escalate. You might even add, "The two of you need to work this out on your own."

3. If the younger child is an infant and cannot protect herself, of course you must be responsible. Be sure the older child cannot get to her and hurt her. Teach the older child, instead, how to nurture and protect the baby. Help the older child feel proud about holding back on anger for the baby's sake.

As the younger child learns how to defend herself—and she will—begin to withdraw from their battles. Let them learn about each other—and they will. Give them the feeling that it is a sign of maturity, something they can be proud of, if they can settle their quarrels independently from you.

At the point where each child can take care of himself or herself, they are less likely to hurt each other when you are away. I do not know of one sibling really hurting another unless the parent was present and involved. The triangle fuels the rivalry.

If there is a real battle and one gets hurt, be sure to comfort both children. The aggressor may be as frightened as the victim. Of course the child who attacks needs limits ("That is not acceptable") and consequences ("You can't play with her anymore until you calm yourself down and apologize"). But these won't have much meaning unless you first help him to understand his feelings, and to find ways of gaining self-control. One parent bought a child a "beating toy"—a life-sized doll he could smash around. "When you feel like hitting your little brother, go find your beating toy and smash it instead. You'll feel better afterward. We all have to learn how to control these feelings. I do every time someone barges ahead of me at the checkout counter. I've learned, and you will too." (See *Understanding Sibling Rivalry: The Brazelton Way*.)

"Spoiled" Children

A child who ends up with the label "spoiled" is one who has never learned his own limits, never learned to entertain and comfort himself. He is likely to have lived in an overprotective or overindulgent environment. Such a child is often a whiny, fussy child who cries a lot.

Is a child who demands attention by crying a "spoiled child"? Crying in the second year, or even in the first year, that is aimed at parents and that has no obvious cause except to demand attention makes everyone wince. An anxious, unresourceful child who exhibits this kind of crying may be labeled as spoiled. Though the demanding crying is aimed at getting a response from adults, its very quality carries a message: "You can't satisfy me."

Some parents may try to do everything for such a child. Perhaps there had been an earlier worry about the child—for example, prematurity, illness, the effect on the child of a family problem. Parents may feel that they have failed the child. Other parents may be trying to make up for feeling that as children they themselves had been failed.

Often, when the child must face another stress, even a small, everyday one, parents rush in too soon. The child will miss out on facing the challenge for himself, facing his frustration and the need to try again. He will miss out on the all-important sense of

"I did it *myself*!" This feeling is critical to his future self-image, his sense of his own competence.

Parents of a child like this need to reconsider their approach. Maybe they aren't leaving enough up to the child. Maybe they are unclear about the limits that this child needs in order to feel loved. I urge the parents of children like this to try the following:

1. Reevaluate your rules and expectations. Then set clear limits and present them with your confident belief that limits help rather than punish your child.
2. Let the child work to experience his own sense of achievement.
3. Identify tasks that will give a child a chance to experience this sense of solving a problem on his own.
4. Turn back the satisfaction for each accomplishment to the child. Instead of "I'm proud of you," substitute "Do you realize what you just did? Aren't *you* proud?"
5. In between episodes of frustration, in order to reassure the child that you are not deserting him, pick him up to show you love him. Then both you and he can feel safer when you push him: "Do it yourself."

Stealing

Just as young children try to change whatever they can't accept about their world by lying, they also are bound to take whatever they can't stand not having. A 2-year-old who sees a toy he wants, made especially appealing because another child is playing with it, will reach out and grab for it. As the other child howls in protest, he will clutch it to his chest and say, "I want it. It's mine." At this age, stealing is easy to handle, because children have not yet learned to feel guilty enough to want to hide what they've done.

This kind of stealing is an important opportunity for learning. Of course the limit needs to be set: "Taking other people's things is not allowed." But so much more must be learned. A child this age needs a parent's help to learn to handle wishes that can't be satisfied, to learn rules about personal belongings, sharing, and taking turns, and to begin to consider the feelings of the child who has been stolen from. These are the goals for discipline, and to accomplish them, a parent's first task is to help the child open himself up to all of this new information. Yelling, frightening the child, or overwhelming the child with guilt won't help, especially since he may have already frightened himself with the power of his own feelings.

After setting the limit, pause and see if he already feels bad enough to give the toy back at this point. If he can give the toy back on his own, encourage him to feel proud of himself, not just for listening to you, but also for wanting to do what *he* knew was right. The long-term goal is for the child to care about doing what is right without being told by a parent.

If the child is still so excited about the toy that he can't let go of it, say, "I can see how badly you want to have that toy, and how sad it will make you feel to have to give it back. But it isn't yours. You didn't ask if you could use it, and you weren't given permission to use it. You need to give it back." In this way you are helping him to understand the feelings that have gone beyond his control. You are also suggesting a way for him to borrow the toy, with permission.

If he still won't give it back, either his longing is overwhelming him or he is ready for a power struggle. In either case, negotiating won't help. Instead, it is time to look him in the eye and firmly tell him, "You need to give the toy back right now. If you can't do that, then I will have to take it from you to give it back to the child you took it from." If he doesn't comply, then you must follow through, and be prepared for his tears and protest. "But it was mine. I wanted it." If he has a tantrum, he will need to settle himself before he is ready to learn from this incident.

Once he does, he needs you to pick him up and comfort him: "I know you wanted that toy so badly. You wanted it so much that you dreamed it could be yours. It is so hard not to have something when you want it so much." As you soothe him you are teaching him how to handle his own upsetting feelings. You are helping him to recognize the feelings that he must face if he is to learn to live in the world, as it is, without lying or stealing as a way of trying to change it. His sobbing will slow down and become softer, and soon he will be ready to listen to the rules and to participate in finding other ways of dealing with his wishes. You might say, "This is your chance to learn that you can't take things that don't belong to you, no matter how much you want them." Stop and see if he looks up at you and into your eyes. Give him a moment to take this in. Then you might ask him to think about how bad he would feel if someone took one of his beloved toys.

Incidents like these are also opportunities for parents to help children learn problem-solving and social skills. Help the child see that wanting someone else's toy is really a problem, and that there might be other ways to solve it. "What else could you try?" He may stare back at you blankly, but if he is ready to listen, you can make a suggestion: "Maybe you could make a trade. You could ask your friend if he wants to try one of your toys if he'll let you use his. Maybe you could ask him to let you borrow it, if you promise to give it back when you're done. Or maybe you could ask if he would let you share it with him for a little while. Then you could find a way to play together with his toy, or you could take turns." Borrowing, taking turns, sharing, and giving and taking are all skills that a child this age needs to learn. Many repetitions of these opportunities for learning will be necessary, but this is an early chance to begin.

If a child is still stuck in sulking—"I just want that toy"—all a parent needs to do, after righting the wrong by returning the object, is to commiserate with him: "It is awfully hard not to have what you want." He is learning to live with the world, not as he wants it to be, but as it is. There will be many more occasions for this learning in the coming years. If each one can be handled calmly and definitively, and the difference between wishful thinking and reality can be pointed out, the goal of honesty can be achieved.

As children get older there may be other reasons for stealing. Always try to see what lies behind the act. Is the child trying to tell you something important? "I feel so lonely, so inadequate. I want to be like other kids, especially the one I stole from." Or, "I need to prove how bad I am so I can be controlled in a safer way. I'm scared and I can't control myself." Or, "There is something important missing in my life and I don't know what it is. So I'll take what I can get."

Even in these cases, the first step is to be clear that the stealing must be faced and won't be tolerated. Then a parent will need to help the child understand his reasons for stealing. "I know you know that it is wrong to take other people's stuff. Do you know why you did it?" Often, a child will not know. If he can accept that this is a question worth thinking about, then he has begun to get control over this behavior. If a child answers, "Because I wanted it. I didn't think I would get caught," this is an important opportunity to help a child think about why people do what is right, even when they don't have to. Understanding this is a major step in any child's development. When an older child seems unreachable, and reasons for continued stealing are not clear, a child may need the help of a child psychotherapist to reach this understanding.

Older children may steal to be part of the gang: "See, I can get this as I walk through a store. I'm cool." It is essential for parents to insist that the child return the stolen item. Otherwise it won't be entirely clear that stealing is unacceptable. But parents may feel desperate and tend to overreact. If parents can see the child's motivation, they can talk to him about it. If the child says, "Everyone steals stuff at the mall," a parent can ask, "Do you really want to be like everyone else?"

Older children who steal may not yet have learned the lessons of earlier years. There are harder lessons to learn as a child gets older. If the limits have not been set earlier and a child has been successful at stealing without penalty, it will be difficult later for a parent to be present in all situations in which the child cannot stop himself. When a child learns early, a parent can expect the child's conscience to be present when a parent cannot be.

Swearing and Toilet Talk

At 4 and 5 years, a child starts to imitate the swearing and toilet talk of his peers, or of his parents. But how can he know that this kind of speech sets off negative reactions in adults? They have been so proud of the way he usually speaks. He is learning new words and phrases daily. When he imitates adults' speech, he is usually rewarded with their praise. All of a sudden, he imitates a dirty word, or swears just like his parent. Everyone stops talking. Their faces darken, or they may laugh. He is overwhelmed by the surprising reactions. He mumbles the word again, to try to see what this reaction is all about. The shocked silence and the overreactions are likely to reinforce the child's new words. Now he can be expected to try them over and over, louder and louder.

After the initial surprise and overreaction, parents would do well to relax—this is experimentation and imitation. They may wonder whether this signifies a sudden interest in toilets, sex, forbidden behaviors. "What's next?" Parents may also wonder whether the child has been molested sexually. All sorts of fears arise. But this experimentation is common and even normal (unless the language is of a detailed, sexually explicit nature that he could not possibly have heard at home or with other children his age).

Don't overreact. If you must comment on it, say, "That kind of talk bothers people. People don't like to listen to it." But the less attention you pay it, the more likely he will be to lose interest and stop. Ask yourself whether the child is modeling the language he hears around him. You may become aware of how often you or your spouse swear or use words that he's imitating.

You may fear that your child is picking up such language from "dirty-mouthed children"—and he may be. But this is not a reason to withdraw him from play dates or from preschool. Instead, use this chance to teach him about how this kind of talk affects other people, and to be sure he cares. If the swearing or toilet talk persists, you may need to make sure he understands that he could offend people when he says these things. Explain why this kind of talk is offensive. You may even need to ask whether that is what he means to do. If he does, it is time to understand what he is angry about, and offer ways to help.

Older children who must resort to such words and to frequent swearing are often insecure and need this kind of language to draw attention to themselves, or to appear older and tough. Praising them for their admirable qualities may be the best way to help them feel less insecure.

In rare cases, a child who swears has no control over what he is saying. Children with Tourette's syndrome, an uncommon neurological disorder, have tics, and swearing can be a kind of tic. But this swearing is different. It is repetitive, comes out of the blue, makes no sense in the context in which it occurs, and is usually accompanied by other tics—repetitive tics or grimaces or movements of the arms or legs.

Talking Back

"Why don't you go clean *your* room?" demanded an angry child who was asked to clean his. A child who talks back is uncertain about his role and that of his parents. He may not accept his parents' authority. A child who says, "I don't have to and you can't make me," needs to find out how his parents can help him keep himself in control. He may be testing, asking for his parents to reassure him that they will set limits when needed, and that they won't put up with talking back.

A child who talks back may feel threatened or criticized by something that has just been said to him. Perhaps he has misunderstood, and is not able to learn from what was said. Perhaps he understood all too well, took it personally, and in the moment is using words to fight back. A parent who says, "Once in a while

you need to think about someone other than yourself," is saying
something important, but too directly and too harshly for a child
to hear. The child might angrily reply, "I do not. You're the one
who needs to think about someone other than *your*self!" Right
now he can't hear what his parent has to say. Talking back pushes
the parent's painful comments as far away as possible. But later,
the child may take those difficult words to heart.

There are several questions to ask about a child who talks back.
Does he feel powerless and never listened to, or too powerful, and
scared that no one seems to be ready to help him keep himself in
control? Does he really understand the effects of what he says on
other people, and has anybody helped him see how talking back
makes other people feel? What kind of talk goes on around him?
How much sarcasm and fighting is he regularly exposed to?

Ways to limit talking back:

1.   First, set the limit: "Talking that way is not acceptable."
2.   When the child protests, or falls apart, pull back and wait
     for him to settle himself down before trying to help him
     learn about how to communicate. He may even need a
     moment of silence, or some time alone in his room. Then
     a cuddle, or some gentle humor.
3.   Be sure he learns that talking this way will not get him
     what he wants. Don't respond to his demand. "When you
     talk like that to people, they aren't going to listen. But as
     soon as you are ready to change your tone of voice, I'll be
     glad to hear what you have to say."
4.   Suggest more effective ways of talking if he can't seem
     to find these on his own. "It is okay for you to disagree
     about some things. But tell me why you disagree so that

I really understand. Even if I can't change my mind, I do want to know what you think. Maybe we still won't be able to do what you want, but I could help you understand why."

5. Make sure the child knows what talking back is and what effect it has on others. "When you say things like that (or when you talk with that tone of voice), you make people angry. Or you hurt their feelings. They won't want to listen to you." Use humor and talk with a cartoon voice to get him to think about how people react to different tones of voice—as long as he knows you are not making fun of him.

6. Give him a chance to apologize and try again: "Are you ready to say you're sorry for being rude?" "Are you ready to try to tell me what you have to say with different words (or a different voice)?"

Tantrums

Tantrums generally begin in the second year. So much learning and hard work go into this year—for the toddler and for parents. I would change the label of the "terrible twos" to "terrific twos." When the toddler begins to walk and "disappear" around a corner, he has set out to explore his universe on his own. He begins to feel the excitement of his independence. But it carries a frightening cost. "Will Daddy be there if I can't see him as I 'disappear' around the corner?" "Did Mommy really get mad at me for climbing the stairs alone?" This cost is written on the toddler's face as he explores. He nearly always looks back to see whether a parent is watching as he sets out on his expeditions.

The child's mixed feelings about independence often have no apparent trigger, leaving parents puzzled. "Why did he fall apart?" Often, being torn between two opposite wishes, or between wanting independence and being scared of it, is what's underneath the 2-year-old's tantrum. He wants so much to be his own boss. Let him settle his own decision, if you can. Value his spirited attempt to make his own decision. The more you do to help him, the more upset he'll be. Don't try to stop it. You'll just make it worse. Just walk away, if he's in a safe place. After he's back in control, pick him up to love him and to say, "It's really tough to make up your mind, isn't it? But you decided yourself."

A temper tantrum is a child's issue, not a parent's. They must leave it to him to settle his internal questions: "Will I or won't I?" "Do I want or don't I?" What sets a tantrum off seems so trivial and unexpected to a parent, but it obviously has real significance for the toddler. For a parent, the child's feeling of helplessness, of loss of control, is matched with a tendency to lose control oneself. Child abuse can occur in the second year as a result of the adult anguish that these tantrums cause. When these tantrums occur in public places, as they are likely to, parents feel exposed as "bad parents." Unable to help or to stop the insistent wailing and thrashing, they feel helpless, inadequate, even guilty. Every onlooker adds to this as they stand and glare at the parent and screeching child. I have found that the surest way to end such an episode is to turn one's back on the scene. When you walk away (if he's safe) or stop reacting in an overt way, the force of the tantrum is lost. You are saying, "You can handle this yourself."

When it is over, return to pick the child up and hug him, saying, "It feels terrible to get so upset." In this way, let him know you accept him as he is. You can even understand the inner turmoil he is experiencing. In a way, you are also saying, "I wish I could help you, but I can't." And indeed, it is his inner struggle to make decisions himself rather than depending on a parent that triggers the tantrum. Stepping back to let him settle himself is a little like encouraging him to soothe himself—for example, with a teddy bear or with his thumb. When he discovers that he can master these feelings, he will feel less at their mercy.

Parents ask whether they can avoid tantrums by making light of each issue *before* the child gets too overwhelmed. Humor and picking your battles are important. But a child realizes when you are protecting him and may feel undermined. Placating a toddler surely won't help him learn to manage the tortured decision making that led to these tantrums. Taking this step toward independence is his most important job in the second year.

A child who continues to have frequent tantrums after age 5, or a child who has frequent, prolonged tantrums (more than 20 to 30 minutes), may be coping with an underlying fragility that requires evaluation by your pediatrician, and sometimes referral to a specialist.

Tattling

A child who tattles faces a moral dilemma. Do I betray my friend's trust? Or do I remain silent about a wrongdoing?

When the misdeed does not really require adult intervention, the ideal solution would be for the child to help the other child see his error and change his ways. Though this may ask more of a young child than he is ready for, it is a worthy goal to suggest. This will help him to see that when a tattler tells all to win a parent's praise, he won't.

A child who tattles shouldn't be rewarded. But should he be punished? The child's dilemma should certainly be acknowledged. A parent who is overly grateful for the information the child supplies, though, is bound to reinforce the tattling. Limiting praise and helping him to see how his tattling will interfere with his friendships are probably enough. Let him ponder how to handle such situations without hurting a friend. A parent has succeeded when a child who tattles is ready to consider alternatives. To help him imagine the pride in himself that he'd feel if he could stand up to his friend on his own. Despite all this, children should be encouraged to confide in an adult when another child's behaviors threaten their own safety or that of other children. Revelations like these are not tattling!

Teasing

All children tease. It is a form of communication that is difficult for anyone who is being teased to ignore. Sooner or later most children learn that teasing is a sure way to get another child to pay attention. They will discover that there is power in teasing. It is likely to cause a stir when the other child gets teased to the point of breaking down. Teasing can be a form of dominating the other child, especially a younger brother or sister. It can even be fun, if the other child can tease back. But teasing that hurts needs to be addressed.

1. Try to understand the underlying reason for the teasing. Is the child who teases insecure? Does he need to dominate in order to feel secure? Or is teasing a way of establishing the pecking order? Does he have trouble making friends and

getting along with other children? Is he desperately trying to get the other child's attention? Is he reacting to something that is different about the other child that he doesn't understand and that frightens him?

2. Tell him he must stop: "You need to stop teasing. It hurts other people's feelings." If he can't, try to distract him to see how strong his need to tease is.

3. If he still won't stop, pick him up or hold him firmly, and remove him from his "victim."

4. When the child has quieted and can be reached, hold him and talk to him: "No one likes to be teased like that. What were you trying to do?" He may not know. He may not be able to say. You might have to tell him, "If you don't like that child, you don't have to play together. If you do want to be friends, try playing a game with him and getting to know him without teasing."

5. Suggest that he try to imagine how it feels to be teased like that, so that he can get himself ready to apologize. Can he say "I'm sorry I hurt your feelings" and really mean it? Help him see that he can feel proud of himself, instead of humiliated, when he does apologize.

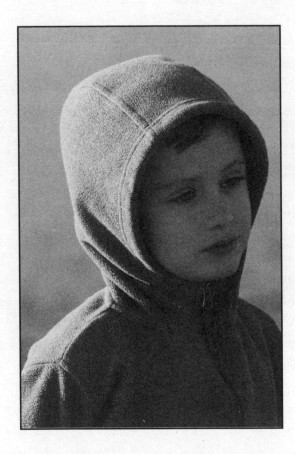

CHAPTER SIX

Common Disciplinary Challenges

Digital Technology

Digital media can open a new window into virtual worlds for a child. But they present parents with two disciplinary tasks: setting limits both on the amount of time children spend using them and on the kinds of content and activities they engage in. Digital devices are merely tools. Whether they are good, bad, or without influence on children will depend on how often they are used, how they are used, and what they are used for. Parents can monitor and help make their child's use of digital technology positive by taking some time to play with the device with the child, and to talk with the child about what she thinks of it and what she is learning.

Like television and video games, most screen-based activities using smart phones, tablets, and computers are sedentary, and, as a result, present a risk for unhealthy weight gain. When considering the possible risks of such attractive and compelling technologies, it is important to look not only at the potential harms that they might cause directly, but also at those that may be caused indirectly when they replace important regular activities. Children need time not only for exercise, but also for play, social interaction, chores, and all kinds of other pursuits that help them develop a range of interests and skills that screen-based activities alone won't build.

Young children need parents to protect them from the potential dangers arising from some of the content and interactions that digital technology delivers. It is critical to block access to "adults-only" websites and to sites and social media where predatory adults may attempt to contact your child. If it is not possible to block access, then you must supervise the child's use of any device that connects to the Internet until the child is old enough to understand and respect the potential dangers, and can demonstrate that she can do so.

Limits

The American Academy of Pediatrics recommends limiting children's screen time as much as possible, or entirely, before 2 years of age, and to no more than 2 hours per day thereafter. Here are a few simple steps to make it easier to stick to these recommendations:

1. Don't offer the use of tablets or smart phones as a reward, and don't take them away as a punishment. Either way, this will make them seem too special, and struggles will result when it is time to stop.
2. Don't use tablets and smart phones as the first or most frequent form of distraction and entertainment for your

child. If you do, your child will find it much harder to learn other ways to entertain herself, and, again, the struggles when it is time to stop will be much more intense.

3. Do store digital devices out of children's reach. It is up to you to decide when it is time to use them, and when that time is over.

4. Try to limit your own use of these devices when in your child's presence. Your child looks up to you, wants to do everything just the way you do, and is watching you more closely than you may realize.

Alternatives and Positive Uses of Technology

Most important of all, expose your child to a range of activities—sports and games involving other kinds of toys and objects—and, of course, people. Children who learn to find pleasure in a rich and varied array of things to do and people to be with will be far less dependent on digital technology, and easier to wean from it when they reach their daily maximum time limit. Children are scientists who use all of their senses—their whole bodies—to explore and learn. They do best when they can follow their curiosity and invent their own tools for discovering their world.

Young children need help (from parents, teachers, child librarians) to find fun and exciting digital activities that are educational and developmentally appropriate. This will help decrease the risk of straying to inappropriate sites and activities. The best digital technology toys for children allow them to program the technology, rather than the other way around. Teachers and child librarians may be able to suggest digital toys and activities that children use in active rather than passive ways.

Health Issues

When a child is sick, she is bound to regress. Of course she'll need you to hug her and hold her and let go of some of your usual expectations for her. You'll feel better too when you are able to give her comfort in these ways. You'll both bounce back to normal quickly when the illness is mild and short-lived. But with a chronic illness, so much can get thrown out of whack.

With any serious illness, the whole family will have to make adjustments: routines and schedules may have to be changed to fit doctors' appointments and treatments; some school may have to be missed; urgent symptoms may drain everyone's energy and focus all of the attention on the sick child. When the illness drags on, the child is bound to tire of it and all the limitations it brings. Sometimes, being babied may not feel comforting, but like one more reminder of the cost of being sick.

Consistent expectations for a sick child can make her feel like less of a baby and more "'normal," even if some of them need to be scaled down to fit restrictions on what she can do. Insisting on the same mutual respect that family members have always been held to will also help protect her self-respect: it feels awful to behave badly, no matter how sick one is. She may also be grateful for opportunities to participate in the family's daily routines and chores, even if these are limited to gestures like folding some laundry or planning a meal. This can help a child find her way back to being her old self again—or as close to this as she can get.

No rules at all for the sick child can feel like a loss of hope. Choosing and upholding appropriate ones that fit the child's special situation may take more time and energy than parents of a sick child may feel they have. But the child will appreciate the extra care you have taken to establish the right kind of rules for her, no matter how much she grouses about them. Just don't expect her to thank you. Still, she's likely to sense that her identity has not been reduced to that of the sick child, and that she can still join in with the family in these ways.

You may need to have a different set of rules for your sick child and your healthy ones. If so, you'll need to explain to all of them that fairness is not a one-size-fits-all affair.

Academic Pressures

With all the emphasis on school readiness, too many preschool and kindergarten teachers are pressured into imposing classwork that is more appropriate for first graders and older children. All too often, getting an early start is misunderstood to mean using curriculum, requirements, and teaching styles with younger children that are similar to those used with older ones.

Children who are 3 and 4 years old do not learn exactly the same way that 5- and 6-year-olds do. Even more than these older children, they learn with all their senses, their whole bodies, and on their feet. While older children are more focused on exploring the mechanics of the real world, 3- and 4-year-olds are still trying to figure out what is real and what is not. They use play and their imaginations to learn about themselves, each other, and their world. Without rich and stimulating opportunities to do this, boredom can lead to misbehavior just as too much pressure can.

The daily rhythms of small children are different too. They need more and longer breaks, and more physical activity. Their attention spans are shorter. Classroom activities that take all of this into account will help them develop the character skills—for

example, persistence, perseverance, flexibility, frustration tolerance, motivation to learn—that will help them succeed as learners
throughout life.

Pushing young children to learn the way older ones do won't
work. Instead, it's likely to backfire, and may turn some children
against school. Through their fidgeting, daydreaming, tantrums,
refusal to comply, and efforts to avoid schoolwork or even school,
some young children are sending parents and teachers a message:
long periods of sitting at desks, writing in workbooks, filling in
sheets, memorizing by rote, and taking tests just aren't the way
they learn.

While there is no excuse for misbehavior, as we said earlier, it
is important to listen to what children's behavior is saying. When
it is telling us that they are being pressed to learn in developmentally inappropriate ways, it's time to let up on the pressure and
reconsider what we're doing to them. Of course, no parent alone
can fix the educational system. Nor can a single teacher. But this
is one instance in which we must we ask which changes in early
education are helping and which ones are hurting.

Economic Pressures on Families

In tough economic times, many parents are forced to take on
extra work, sometimes working two or more jobs, or taking night
courses when still working during the day. Children may have to
fill in some of the gaps at home. As long as the chores they must
take on are within their abilities given their ages, do not endanger
them, and do not interfere with the time they need for schoolwork
and for play, helping out for the family's sake can be a positive
and rewarding experience for the child. This is more likely when

others in the child's life—teachers, relatives, friends, and their parents—see this as a positive too.

Chores can be fun, but they aren't always, and entertainment is not their main purpose. So of course children will grumble, slack off, and try to avoid chores—in ever more creative ways as they mature. Such misbehavior can be expected, and consistently responded to.

Sometimes, a neutral, matter-of-fact reminder of the consequence for failure to complete the chore is best: "We're just going to have to wait for you to set the table before we can sit down and eat." Sometimes, gentle encouragement and a bit of light humor that shows you do understand how she's feeling can help: "I know this isn't your favorite thing to do, but we're almost done, and when we are, we can look for some even more boring things to do!"

When are chores too much? When the struggles become constant, and start to invade your relationship with your child and your interactions with each other, then it may be time to pull back and reassess. If your child is expected to help out more than others in the neighborhood, you may simply need to listen openly to her questions and concerns about this. If the problem is that there are just too many chores for her to handle, or ones that really are too hard for her at her age, adjust them. But don't get rid of chores altogether. If you do, you'll be rewarding the fussing and whining. Instead, you might simply say it's time to switch and try some new ones, and pick a few that are less demanding and take a bit less time to complete.

Grandparents and Discipline

Discipline is usually not a grandparent's main concern. "It's so much easier to be a grandparent than a parent. My job is to spoil my grandchildren rotten and to let my children see what it's like to have to discipline them!" Although their job may not actually be to spoil them, when grandparents don't have to raise their grandchildren, they can simply enjoy them, listen to them, and appreciate them. Also, they can add to their grandchildren's sense of who they are by giving them a sense of the family they come from.

Grandparents are indeed right in leaving the parenting to parents. They can defer to parents' rules and expectations, and, at the very least, should avoid undermining them. My children made it perfectly clear to me that with their children it was their turn to make their own mistakes. "Dad, stay out of it," they would say. That can be hard for grandparents to do, especially when they see their children struggling to find their way as parents, but probably it is still the best advice.

If absolutely necessary, a grandparent can say, "When you're with your parents, you need to follow their rules, but when you're with me, you'll need to follow mine." It may be surprising, but by 4 or 5 years of age, most children are already able to accept and respect the differences, especially when parents and grandparents show that they respect each other's rules. Children may question some rules in order to try to have the ones they prefer applied everywhere ("At Nana's we don't have to do that!"), but they can and will have to accept that "That's okay at her house, but this is the way we do it at ours." Problems most often arise when parents and grandparents openly disapprove of each other's rules. Then children will be caught in a bind. Obeying one set of adults may seem to betray the other set. The children will test the rules until the adults can reach agreement, or agree to disagree without putting the children in the middle.

Discipline is a bigger concern for the many grandparents who are actually raising their grandchildren. For many parents, childcare is unaffordable or of poor quality. Many parents must work two or more jobs, or spend more time commuting or even live in different cities in order to find and keep work. Such parents may need their parents' help. Others may turn to their parents when they are raising their children alone, when they are working and going to school at the same time, or when they are struggling with mental health challenges or substance use.

When grandparents have taken on the role of primary caregivers, there can be no retreating from the disciplinary role. On the contrary: if their children have not been able to care for their children as they would have wanted to, grandparents may need to be especially firm and clear.

Children may challenge grandparents who have become their main caregivers out of a sense of loyalty to their parents: "I don't have to do what you say. You're not even my mommy!" Very young children may be confused when they are moved from a parent's to grandparents' care. Some limit testing can be expected as children struggle to find out, "Am I going to Grandma's because I was bad? She doesn't get to tell me what to do."

Withholding discipline will only make all of this worse. Every child needs to know that whoever is taking care of her cares enough to discipline her and put up with the inevitable protests that result.

Single Parents

Discipline can be challenging for single parents because they feel they have to play two roles. "I have to be the mother *and* the father. There is no one to back me up, to talk things over with, or just unload with. I'm the nurturer and the disciplinarian. There's no one to share all the 'no's' with. There's no chance just to have fun."

Often, discipline can be even harder for single parents when their feelings of guilt or inadequacy get in the way. Many worry that their child is missing out on not having two parents, and blame themselves. They're bound to hold back on discipline, at least at times, as if that could make up for whatever they and their children feel might be missing. Yet when children receive the discipline that any child needs, many who grow up in single-parent families can learn to feel proud of their own self-reliance and of the way their family works together as a team. When single parents can see glimpses of these positive adaptations, it is easier for them to let up on themselves, and to deliver discipline with less hesitation and greater certainty.

Single parents may feel that no one can replace a partner in the home. Many eventually realize, though, that their children are soaking up as much as they can from all of the other adults in their lives—grandparents, aunts, uncles, neighbors, teachers, and their friends' parents. With luck, individuals can be found who share similar values, and help create a broader shared sense of the standards a single parent expects the child to live up to. Some may serve as positive role models. Single parents may also find adults they can talk to about the behavior problems they are dealing with, and the solutions they are considering. With this kind of communication, some of these adults may even be enlisted to join the kind of united front that children raised in two-parent families need—and don't always have.

Bibliography

Baumrind, Diana. *Child Maltreatment and Optimal Caregiving in Social Contexts.* New York: Garland, 1995.

Brazelton, T. B. *Infants and Mothers,* revised edition. New York: Delacorte Press, 1994.

Brazelton, T. B. *Parents and Toddlers,* revised edition. New York: Delacorte Press, 1989.

Brazelton, T. B., and Sparrow, J. D. *Mastering Anger and Aggression: The Brazelton Way.* Boston: Da Capo Press, 2005.

Brazelton, T. B., and Sparrow, J. D. *Touchpoints Birth to Three: Your Child's Emotional and Behavioral Development,* revised edition. Boston: Da Capo Press, 2006.

Brazelton, T. B., and Sparrow, J. D. *Touchpoints Three to Six: Your Child's Emotional and Behavioral Development.* Cambridge, MA: Perseus Publishing, 2001.

Brazelton, T. B., and Sparrow, J. D. *Understanding Sibling Rivalry: The Brazelton Way.* Boston: Da Capo Press, 2005.

Canada, Geoffrey. *Fist, Stick, Knife, Gun: A Personal History of Violence in America.* Boston: Beacon Press, 1996.

Chess, Stella, and Thomas, Alexander. *Know Your Child: An Authoritative Guide for Today's Parents.* New York: Basic Books, 1987.

Comer, James P., and Poussaint, Alvin F. *Raising Black Children: Two Leading Psychiatrists Confront the Educational, Social and Emotional Problems Facing Black Children.* New York: Penguin, 1992.

Fraiberg, Selma H. *The Magic Years: Understanding and Handling the Problems of Early Childhood.* New York: Scribner, 1959.

Galinsky, Ellen. *The Preschool Years: Family Strategies That Work—from Experts and Parents.* New York: Ballantine Books, 1991.

Ginott, Hiam G. *Between Parent and Child: New Solutions to Old Problems.* New York: MacMillan, 1971.

Gold, Claudia M. *Keeping Your Child in Mind.* Boston: Da Capo Press, 2011.

Greene, Ross W. *The Explosive Child: A New Approach for Understanding and Parenting Easily Frustrated, "Chronically Inflexible" Children.* New York: HarperCollins, 1998.

Greenspan, Stanley. *Building Healthy Minds: The Six Experiences That Create Intelligence and Emotional Growth in Babies and Young Children.* Boston: Da Capo Press, 2000.

Greenspan, Stanley. *The Challenging Child: Understanding, Raising, and Enjoying the Five "Difficult" Types of Children.* Cambridge, MA: Perseus Publishing, 1996.

Johnson, Robert L., and Stanford, Paulette. *Strength for Their Journey: Five Essential Disciplines African American Parents Must Teach Their Children and Teens.* New York: Harlem Moon Broadway Books, 2002.

Kindlon, Dan. *Too Much of a Good Thing: Raising Children of Character in an Indulgent Age.* New York: Talk Miramax Books, 2001.

Kranowitz, Carol Stock. *The Out-of-Sync Child: Recognizing and Coping with Sensory Processing Disorder,* revised edition. New York: Skylight Press, 2005.

Mogel, Wendy. *The Blessing of a Skinned Knee: Using Jewish Teachings to Raise Self-Reliant Children.* New York: Scribner, 2001.

Robinson, Ricki G. *Autism Solutions: How to Create a Healthy and Meaningful Life for Your Child.* Don Mills, Ontario: Harlequin, 2011.

Westman, Jack, ed. *Parenthood in America: Undervalued, Underpaid, Under Siege.* Madison: University of Wisconsin Press, 2001.

Resources for Parents

American Academy of Pediatrics
P.O. Box 927
Elk Grove, IL 60009
(847) 434-4000
www.aap.org
Write for the Parent Resource Guide or pediatrician referrals.

Campaign for a Commercial-Free Childhood
89 South St., Ste. 403
Boston, MA 02111
(617) 896-9368
www.commercialfreechildhood.org

Media Lab at Massachusetts Institute of Technology
The Lab has several groups working on interactive, innovative programs for children. Among these are the Lego group, the Scratch group, and the Center for Future Children.
www.medialab.mit.edu

Parents Anonymous
675 W. Foothill Blvd., Ste. 250
Claremont, CA 91711
(909) 621-6184
www.parentsanonymous.org

Healthy Families America
228 S. Wabash
Chicago, IL 60604
(312) 663-3520
www.healthyfamiliesamerica.org

National Child Abuse Hotline
(800) 422-4453

Parents Action for Children
4117 Hillsboro Pike, Ste. 103–130
Nashville, TN 37215
www.parentsaction.org
Write for a discipline videotape.

Brazelton Touchpoints Center
Boston Children's Hospital
1295 Boylston St., Ste. 320
Boston, MA 02115
(617) 355-6000
www.brazeltontouchpoints.org

Acknowledgments

We would like to thank Richard and Tivia Kramer and the residents of the Harlem Children's Zone for having first urged us to write this concise, accessible book on a topic of the utmost importance to parents around the country, for without their vision it might never have been written. Thanks also go to Geoffrey Canada, Marilyn Joseph, Karen Lawson and her late husband Bart, David Saltzman, and the late Caressa Singleton for their unwavering support for our work, and from whom we have learned so much. We would also like to thank our Native American colleagues who have shared with us the ways in which discipline is taught in their cultures.

As always, we would again like to thank our editor, Merloyd Lawrence, for her wisdom and guidance. Finally, we wish to express our gratitude to the many families with whom we have worked who have taught us so much, and to our families, not only for their encouragement and patience, but also for the lessons they have taught us that we have sought to impart in this book.

Index

About the Authors

T. Berry Brazelton, MD, founder of the Child Development Unit at Boston Children's Hospital, is Clinical Professor of Pediatrics Emeritus at Harvard Medical School. His many important and popular books include the internationally best-selling *Touchpoints* and *Infants and Mothers*. A practicing pediatrician for over fifty years, Dr. Brazelton founded two programs at Children's Hospital: the Brazelton Institute (www.brazelton-institute.com) and the Brazelton Touchpoints Center (www.brazeltontouchpoints.org), which further his work nationally and internationally.

Joshua D. Sparrow, MD, is Associate Professor (part-time) of Psychiatry at Harvard Medical School, and Director at the Brazelton Touchpoints Center in the Division of Developmental Medicine at Boston Children's Hospital. He is the coauthor, with Dr. Brazelton, of *Touchpoints Three to Six*, and the Brazelton Way series—*Sleep*, *Calming Your Fussy Baby*, *Feeding Your Child*, *Toilet Training*, *Mastering Anger and Aggression*, and *Understanding Sibling Rivalry*—and coeditor, with Barry Lester, of *Nurturing Children and Families: Building on the Legacy of T. Berry Brazelton*. Dr. Sparrow also revised with Dr. Brazelton *Touchpoints: Birth to Three*, for its fifteenth anniversary edition.